Liszt

THE GREAT COMPOSERS

LISZT

by

ALAN WALKER

FABER AND FABER

3 Queen Square

London

First published in 1971
by Faber and Faber Limited
Printed in Great Britain by
Latimer Trend & Co Ltd Plymouth

ISBN 0 571 09120 2

© Alan Walker 1971

Contents

Illustrations

Music Examples

A Note on the Music Examples

Liszt's music, especially that composed during his middle years, is often difficult to play. Works like *Mazeppa* (p. 35) and the 'Dante' Sonata (p. 42) will forever lie beyond the powers of all but the true virtuoso. Anyone who listens to just a few of the gramophone records mentioned in the Discography, however, will have some idea of what Liszt stands for in the world of piano playing. Rubinstein spoke for everyone when he said: 'In comparison with Liszt, all other pianists are children.'

There are many works by Liszt which are well within reach of the young pianist, and anyone wishing to explore Liszt's music at the keyboard will find some fairly simple pieces among the *Years of Pilgrimage* (twenty-six works in three volumes), the Christmas-tree Suite, the six *Consolations*, and the seven *Hungarian Historical Portraits*.

All the music examples are taken from the 'official' text of the *Collected Edition of Liszt's Works*, published by Breitkopf and Härtel during the years 1901–36 under the distinguished editorship of Busoni, Bartók, Motta and Raabe, among others.

I

The Young Prodigy

Liszt was nearly not born. His mother fell down a disused well on the Esterháza estate in Hungary while she was still pregnant, and she was brought up hours later shocked and bruised and soaked to the skin. Right up to her confinement the local doctor at Oedenburg feared the worst; but the child was eventually delivered without complications on Friday, 22 October 1811. That evening, a brilliant comet which had dominated the night skies of Europe ever since the previous August glowed with peculiar luminosity until night was almost turned into day. Astronomers still refer to it as the 'Great Comet' of 1811. People gazed heavenwards, awestruck by this wondrous sight. They took it to be an omen. Many thought the end of the world was at hand. Napoleon was more optimistic. He actually proceeded to plan his disastrous military campaign against Russia, taking it to be a sign of an eventual military victory. Meanwhile, a small group of gipsies encamped outside the tiny village of Raiding in Hungary, who, to judge by later events, were obviously in better practice than Napoleon at predicting the future, foretold a glittering career for Franz Liszt.

As a child, Liszt was told that story so often that it bestowed on him a sense of destiny which he carried to the grave.

Contrary to popular opinion, Liszt had very little Hungarian blood in him. His parents came of Austro-German stock. Even the family name was German, being spelled 'List'—not an uncommon name in Germany—and this is how Liszt's name was entered in the baptismal registry at Raiding. In later life, Liszt said that his father had added a 'z' to the name in order to avoid the Magyar pronunciation 'Lischt'.

His father, Adam Liszt, was a land steward on the estates of Prince Nicholas Esterházy, the same Prince who had been Haydn's benefactor until a few years previously. Adam's father before him had also been a land steward for the Esterházys, and he seems to have had some hereditary claim to the post. He would probably have preferred to become a musician. There is some evidence to suggest that he was talented. As a young man he played the piano and the cello, and he also composed a *Te Deum* which he dedicated to Prince Nicholas. But his youthful ambitions came to nothing, and he eventually followed in his father's footsteps, a frustrated man. In 1810 he was promoted to the village of Raiding to look after the Esterháza properties there. Just before he set out, he married Anna Lager, a native of Lower Austria, and together they journeyed to the small dwelling-house in Raiding that was to be their home for the next ten years. Franz was born within a year of their arrival.

As a child Franz was very delicate, and he suffered from frequent bouts of ill health. He seems also to have had cataleptic seizures which must have been a permanent worry to his parents. It is hardly surprising that they adopted a highly protective attitude towards him. He led a sheltered existence and had few friends of his own age; only a handful of people lived in Raiding. By normal standards, then, his childhood might be described as extremely lonely, were it not for one fact. Franz was far from being a normal boy.

From the start he revealed a prodigious musical talent. It was as if music were his native tongue. By the time he was five years old he had instinctively found his way to the piano; he could improvise long before he could read notation. Adam immediately recognized in his son a phenomenal talent, and it is to his credit that he set about developing it sensibly and systematically. He was able to show the boy how to hold his hands on the keyboard, to teach him to read music and to correct his mistakes during performance; above all, he set before him the entire range of piano music, as it then existed, including Clementi, Mozart, Hummel and even early Beethoven. Soon the father's presence became a mere formality. No sooner was Franz told anything than he seemed to know it already. Before long there was nothing else Adam could teach him. It became necessary to find the boy a teacher worthy of his genius. But where to look? The nearest city was Vienna, and one of the greatest piano teachers of the day, Karl Czerny, was living there. But this would take money, and Adam's salary was small. There was only one thing to do, and Adam was shrewd enough to do it. A concert was arranged for Franz to display his powers in public. That way, if they were lucky, a benefactor might be found.

The first time Liszt appeared before an audience was in 1820, when he was nine years old, at Oedenburg. He shared the concert with a certain Baron von Braun, a blind pianist, who had himself been an infant prodigy

Above, Liszt's parents, Anna and Adam

Below, the composer's birthplace at Raiding, after a drawing by F. Grünes

Left, Liszt in 1832 by A. Devéria; *below*, a kiss from Beethoven after Liszt's piano recital at the age of eleven

but was now out of favour with the public. It was the Baron's idea that Liszt should share the programme with him, thinking, no doubt, that he might in this way pack the house with people curious to see the latest 'nine day wonder' and then seize the opportunity to recapture his lost following by a superior display of talent. He lived to regret the idea. Franz's success was so overwhelming that he stole the show. Adam was now encouraged to put on a concert of his own in Pressburg. It was here that the boy was really launched on his career as a virtuoso. We are told that he roused the audience to a pitch of frenzy by his performance of a difficult concerto by Ries, and by a remarkable improvisation on a theme invited from the audience. Such was the success of the concert that it reached the ears of Prince Nicholas, and Adam was invited to take the boy to Eisenstadt so that the court could hear this wonder for themselves. There, too, Franz created a sensation. He was fussed over by the bejewelled ladies, given a purse of gold and a pat on the head by the Prince, and then presented with a valuable 'name-book' by the Princess which had belonged to Haydn who had collected in its pages the signatures of most of the eminent musicians then living in Europe. It was a priceless volume to give to a small boy, and he soon lost it. But the concert did have a more permanent outcome. Some of the noblemen present agreed to put up a sum of money for the next six years sufficient to enable Liszt to pursue his studies abroad. This magnanimous gesture Liszt never forgot. Adam requested, and received, leave of absence from his post during which time he was to settle the boy with a suitable teacher. Flushed with success, father and son returned to Anna at Raiding, broke the good news to her, packed their belongings, and the entire family then boarded the stage-coach for Vienna. It was to be many years before Franz returned to Hungary; and when he did so, he had shaken the world with his genius.

Arrived in Vienna, and armed with various letters of introduction, Adam set about finding a teacher for his son. His first thought was Hummel who had connections with the court at Eisenstadt and was highly regarded by the Esterházys; unfortunately, he had just taken up an appointment in Weimar. We may be thankful that this was so. Hummel and the young Liszt stood for totally different things. It is likely that Liszt's intuitive and completely natural approach to the keyboard might have suffered irreparable harm under Hummel's dry, pedantic teaching. In later life, in fact, Hummel's family held Liszt responsible for the serious decline in 'the true art of piano playing', evidence of the distance separating the styles of

B

performance the two musicians represented. And so Adam turned to Czerny. The choice was perfect. Czerny had been a pupil of Beethoven and his fame, both as a pianist and as a teacher, was spreading rapidly. Although only thirty years old, a series of brilliant pupils had already passed through his hands, including the astonishing child prodigy Ninette von Bellville who eventually made her master's name resound in all the capitals of Europe.

Adam picked a bad time to approach Czerny who was grossly overworked and not disposed to take any more pupils. He was a bachelor and lived in his parents' house where he taught, sometimes for ten hours a day. His industry was staggering. Apart from his heavy teaching programme, and his being besieged by would-be pupils from every country, he still found time to compose no fewer than 1,000 opuses, many of which consist of fifty numbers or more. His works covered every branch of keyboard technique, and there was little about piano playing that he did not understand. It was only with the greatest reluctance that Czerny agreed to hear the boy play at all; and he granted the audition only on the strict understanding that there was to be no question of regular lessons. It was one of those historic encounters which one wishes were documented more fully, for it was fraught with consequences for both master and pupil. Czerny was determined not to take Liszt as his pupil; Liszt was equally determined that Czerny should become his master. Already, Liszt had worked his way through most of Czerny's studies, and he knew the *School of Velocity* by heart. As the boy composed himself at the keyboard Czerny must have observed the look of bliss fall across his face; it was a look that many later observers commented on, and it showed the intense love-affair which existed between the young boy and the instrument. Liszt started to play, with Czerny looking on. As the crystal clear passage-work rang out Czerny knew that he was listening to a potential master. (Czerny later described the scene in his autobiography: 'It was as if Nature herself had intended him as a pianist.') All objections to accepting Franz as a pupil were now swept aside; after the first few lessons, in fact, he offered to teach the boy for nothing. Adam was overjoyed at the decision, and the family now prepared themselves for a lengthy stay in the Austrian capital.

Master and pupil were perfectly adapted to each other. Czerny's thoughtful and rational approach to the piano was just what the boy needed; it put a healthy check on the spontaneous, almost improvisatory manner which had characterized his playing so far. He was, as we might say today, a 'natural' and he therefore played as the spirit moved him; he would not hesitate to indulge in wild rubatos and even to adorn the composition with embellishments of his own if that was the way he felt the music ought to go. He usually played from memory; in the case of some works he had not looked at the music, quite literally, for years. Czerny made him think about every note. And when necessary he could be a tyrant. He gave the boy massive doses of endurance exercises, forcing him to concentrate on technique for hours on end. For a time, the core of the lessons centred on a systematic study of Clementi's *Gradus ad Parnassum*—a set of bone-breaking exercises which is still a blight on the happiness of piano students everywhere. An adherent of the 'finger equalization' school, Czerny spared no pains to give Liszt a technique that was second to none and which would meet any physical emergency. Although Liszt was with Czerny a mere eighteen months, the benefits of such rigorous training were to remain with him for the rest of his life. It was during these months, in fact, that Liszt laid the foundations for his 'transcendental technique' for which he was later renowned. Years later, when the world was at his feet, he could look back in gratitude to these hours of ungrudging toil which Czerny lavished on him. Long after he had left the Viennese pedagogue, Liszt showed his appreciation in the most direct way possible by dedicating to him his fearsomely difficult '*Transcendental*' *Studies*.

Liszt gave several concerts in Vienna while he was with Czerny, and it was inevitable that sooner or later news of him should reach Beethoven. For months, Adam had busied himself behind the scenes, bringing some diplomatic pressure to bear on Schindler (Beethoven's secretary) for the boy to be presented to Beethoven. But Schindler was cautious. The master detested infant prodigies. Moreover, he was now stone deaf; he found it irritating to hold a conversation with strangers. It was a question of choosing the right moment to broach the matter. Eventually, patience was rewarded and Beethoven agreed, probably out of curiosity, that Schindler should bring the boy to the house. Beethoven's sketch-books have a record of the meeting. The following entry seems to have been written by Franz, or by his father on his behalf.

> I have often expressed the wish to Herr von Schindler to make your high acquaintance, and am rejoiced, now, to be able to do so. As I shall give a concert on Sunday the 13th I most humbly beg you to give me your high presence.

Beethoven's reply, of course, was spoken, so we have no record of it; but he seems to have turned down the invitation in a rather unfriendly manner. A bit later, there is another entry in Schindler's handwriting, evidently written after father and son had left. Schindler, who probably felt guilty about the unfortunate outcome of the meeting, tactfully tried to regain Beethoven's goodwill by playing down Liszt's achievements and blaming Czerny! Again the conversation is one-sided; but it is not difficult to read between the lines and guess the kind of awkward questions Schindler was having to answer.

'Little Liszt has urgently requested me humbly to beg you for a theme on which he wishes to improvise at his concert tomorrow. He will not break the seal till the time comes.'

[Beethoven did not provide this theme.]

'The little fellow's improvisations do not seriously signify.'
'The lad is a fine pianist, but, so far as his fancy is concerned, it is far from the truth to say that he really improvises.'
'Karl Czerny is his teacher.'
'Just eleven years.'
'Do come: it will certainly please Karl to hear how the little fellow plays.'

[Schindler was referring to Beethoven's young nephew, Karl, who appears to have wanted to attend Liszt's concert.]

'It is unfortunate the lad is in Czerny's hands.'
'You will make good the rather unfriendly reception of recent date by coming to the little Liszt's concert. It will encourage the boy. Promise me to come.'

Schindler's tactful replies finally persuaded Beethoven. The following day the great composer turned up at the end of Liszt's concert, mounted the platform as the audience were applauding, and kissed the boy on the forehead. It was a remarkable gesture, and it set the seal on Franz's endeavours. The story has been discredited by some Liszt biographers; but it originated from Liszt himself who had no cause to invent it.

It was while Liszt was studying with Czerny that he published his first known composition. Diabelli, the publisher, had invited fifty of the most distinguished musicians then living in Austria to compose a variation each on a waltz-theme he himself had composed. The resulting collection of variations, which was eventually published by Diabelli, is a fascinating historical document which reflects a great diversity of styles. Liszt, who at this time was eleven, and the youngest contributor, was invited; so, too,

Diabelli's Waltz-theme

Liszt's Variation on Diabelli's Tune

were Schubert, Moscheles, Hummel, Czerny and many other well-known composers, so the request was a great honour for the young boy. Beethoven was also invited, but he refused to have anything to do with Diabelli's theme which he contemptuously dismissed as 'a cobbler's patch'. Later, however, he relented and produced his own independent set of thirty-three variations—possibly the finest set in musical history. Liszt's contribution is of interest because it shows something of Czerny's influence; indeed, it might almost be mistaken for one of Czerny's own piano studies.

It was Czerny who finally decided to break off lessons. After eighteen months he claimed that there was nothing more he could teach Liszt. Already, the twelve-year-old boy was being openly compared with Moscheles

and Hummel, the two greatest pianists of the day. There was now only one place for him to be, and that was Paris, in those days the musical centre of the world. Franz was now beginning to show a flair for composition, and at the Paris Conservatoire he would be able to develop this talent to the full; some of the finest theorists in Europe were on its staff. Adam, with his shrewd head for business, was quick to exploit this new development, and as the family prepared to move to yet another strange city, he set about organizing concerts in all the towns they would visit *en route*—Munich, Stuttgart and Strassburg. Maybe he recalled the highly-publicized tours the young Mozart had made with his father some sixty years earlier; the comparison is an obvious one. People were beginning to link the boy with the young Mozart, and it was typical of Adam to try and symbolize that fact publicly; Franz played in some of the same towns and was greeted with that same mixture of curiosity and excitement which had been a feature of the Mozarts' appearances. He played to full houses, and soon made enough money to cover the family's removal expenses all the way from Vienna to Paris.

The day after their arrival in Paris, Adam and the boy went to the Conservatoire. They carried with them letters of introduction from a number of eminent musicians, including Czerny. At that time, the Director of the Conservatoire was Cherubini. He received them politely enough, read their letters of introduction, and then categorically refused to admit Franz as a student. Father and son were dumbfounded. The rules of the Conservatoire, Cherubini informed them, would not permit foreigners to study there. Although Adam pleaded with him, Cherubini remained quite unbending and refused to allow an exception. He would not even permit Franz to play for him. He seems to have been an unimaginative administrator, blinkered by the rules of office. It was a bitter blow. They were now in a strange city, not knowing a soul, and unable to speak a word of French. They must have regretted leaving Vienna where everyone had been so friendly.

It was while they were pondering what best to do next that they had the good fortune to meet Sébastien Érard. Érard was a famous piano manufacturer, one of the best in Europe. He had followed Liszt's career with great interest for a number of years, and when he heard that the Conservatoire was proving so intractable he made it his business to secure some useful introductions for Franz and he advised Adam on possible teachers for the boy. As a token of his regard for Franz, Érard presented him with a magnificent grand piano, one of the latest to come out of his workshops, a model

24

which incorporated his newly-patented device of the 'double-escapement' which allowed a note to be repeated endlessly without the key having to return each time to its resting position. It represented a major break-through in the development of the piano; Liszt was delighted with this handsome gift whose potential he was quick to recognize.

Eventually, it was Reicha and Paer who became Franz's masters. Reicha had been a pupil of Michael Haydn, Joseph Haydn's younger brother, and was well known as a theorist; Paer, who came from Parma, was a composer of light operas which were very popular during their day. In the circumstances, these arrangements for the boy's future were as satis-factory as could be expected. What was needed now was a public concert to secure his position in the foreign capital.

Liszt made his Paris début on 8 March 1824. It can only be described as sensational.

> I cannot help it; since yesterday evening I am a believer in reincarna-tion. I am convinced that the soul and spirit of Mozart have passed into the body of young Liszt.
>
> His little arms can scarcely stretch to both ends of the keyboard, his little feet scarce reach the pedals, and yet this child is beyond compare; he is the first pianist in Europe. Moscheles himself would not feel offended by this affirmation.
>
> (*Le Drapeau*, 9 March 1824, A. Martainville)

Other concerts quickly followed. Overnight, Paris opened its doors to the boy and he was invited to play in all the leading *salons* of the aristocracy. Everywhere he went, he was lionised and fêted. The windows of the print-shops were full of pictures of the 'little Litz' (the French always had trouble pronouncing his name). At one of his concerts, Gall, the founder of phre-nology, took a cast of the boy's head in order to make a thorough study of it. Soon, as a result of these successes, Adam was able to send a thousand gulden back to Prince Nicholas in part repayment of his help. Franz's future now looked brighter than at any previous time in his career.

But as far as his personal life is concerned, a shadow was cast over it by a serious rift between his parents. Anna had found it increasingly difficult to adapt to her new way of life; she was essentially a simple woman, un-accustomed to wealth, and quite out of her depth, socially, among Adam's newly-acquired circle of acquaintances. She was acutely sensitive about her lowly position, and when it became clear that she would not be able to accompany Adam and Franz on the boy's forthcoming tours, she parted from Adam and went to live with her sister in Styria. Franz, who was devoted to her, must have been distressed by this turn of events which may well have precipitated the nervous illness he was to suffer a couple of years later.

Father and son now began travelling again, starting with London. Liszt played first at the Argyll Rooms on 21 June 1824. This was followed by a concert at Drury Lane in which Franz, according to the posters outside the theatre, 'consented to display his inimitable powers on the New Grand Piano Forte, invented by Sébastien Érard'. The climax to the visit came when they were received by George IV at Carlton House. Franz's playing aroused so much interest that a further visit was arranged next year. This time, Liszt played to George IV at Windsor, and he also played twice in Manchester. Shortly after his return to Paris, just before his fourteenth birthday, his operetta *Don Sanche* was given at the opera house on 17 October 1825 (see page 23). A third visit to England took place the next year in 1827, followed by a tour of the French provinces.

All this unceasing activity was now beginning to tax the boy's health. During the summer months Adam, on doctors' orders, took Franz to Boulogne for sea-baths which were then just becoming fashionable. While they were there, disaster overtook them. Adam fell ill with typhoid fever; he became delirious, and within a few days he was dead. Franz, alone in a strange town, and far from well himself, must have had a wretched time of it; but he nevertheless behaved with remarkable maturity. He supervised the funeral arrangements, paid his father's outstanding debts, and wrote a moving letter to his mother, gently breaking the news of the tragedy to her. Then, having done all he could in Boulogne, he returned to Paris where he had instructed his mother to re-join him. From now on he was to be completely self-supporting. He was fifteen years old.

Once Liszt was settled in Paris, with Anna to look after him, he set about earning a living. The natural thing to do was to teach. And with his reputation he did not have to seek out pupils; they sought him out. The daughters of the fashionable aristocracy were only too glad to own him as a teacher, and this way Liszt was able to keep himself and his mother in comparative comfort.

One of his pupils at this time was a certain Caroline St. Cricq. She was the beautiful sixteen-year-old daughter of the Comte St. Cricq, a man of great wealth who was the Minister of Commerce to Charles X. Franz used to visit the house regularly in order to give the girl lessons, and before long they had formed a passionate attachment for each other. The parents must have known about it for some months later, as the mother lay dying, her last words to her husband were: 'If they love each other, let them be happy.' After the death of his wife, the Comte seemed content to let matters run their own course, and the young couple began to entertain foolish hopes that they might be allowed to marry. Unfortunately, they were discovered by one of the servants prolonging a music lesson far into the night, and the matter was reported to the Comte. A few days later, Franz turned up at the house as usual and was curtly informed that the lessons had been terminated and he was not to be allowed to see Caroline again as it had been arranged for her to marry the Comte d'Artigaux. The blow fell with a shattering impact. Liszt's whole world collapsed about him; he became ill and suffered a nervous breakdown. For the next few months, in fact, he disappeared completely from public view; he lay in a mental torpor, unable to work, totally withdrawn from his surroundings. He succumbed again to the cataleptic seizures that he had suffered from as a child, and it was probably during a particularly severe seizure that the doctors thought he had died. Reports of his death swept Paris, and the French newspaper *L'Étoile* actually carried his obituary notice.

> The young Liszt has died in Paris. At an age when other children do not even think of going to school his talents had conquered the whole world. At the age of nine, when his contemporaries have still an imperfect command of their own language, he—to the astonishment of his teachers— was already improvising at the piano. In spite of this precocity, he was always called 'little Liszt', a name the public linked with the charm of that childhood which he was not long destined to survive.
>
> Liszt's guardian angel was his age, which protected him from every attack. Up to now he had nothing but admirers. 'He is only a child,' people said, and envy remained dormant. If he had grown older and the spark within him had shone more brightly, the critics would have pounced on his faults, sought to diminish his merits, and would perhaps have brought bitterness into his life. He would have had to bear with the whims of destiny, the burdens of injustice, the crudity of attacks motivated by the most basely hostile passions, and these would perhaps have stifled him, whereas now, beneath his shroud, he can prolong his childish dreams for evermore.

Not many people are granted the rare privilege of seeing their own obituary notice in print.

Franz's recovery was slow. He went about like someone in a trance.

During his illness he did not touch the piano for at least a year; in fact, the beautiful grand piano which Érard had given him had now to be sold in order to defray expenses, for no money was coming into the house and all his teaching connections were severed. He remained morbidly introspective and refused to receive visitors. He began to suffer from religious mania and experienced longings to become a priest. One of his few friends at this time was the Abbé Lammenais who became a kind of spiritual father to him. They had many theological discussions together, and it was the good Lammenais who dissuaded Liszt from following his reckless impulse to consign himself to a monastic retreat. Lammenais understood Liszt completely, and saw at once that the young man's excessive religious zeal could not last. Liszt went through a similar spiritual crisis about thirty-five years later, only this time it finally succeeded in bringing him into the priesthood. Another of Liszt's friends was a bizarre character called Christian Urhan who played in the Paris Opera orchestra. Urhan was a man of about forty, and he lived a life of almost Spartan asceticism. His moral principles were said to be so strict that whenever a female dancer appeared on the stage he would play his violin with gaze averted! He appealed to the mystical side of Liszt's personality and they had long discussions lasting far into the night about religion. It was Urhan who introduced Liszt to the Saint-Simonists, a religious sect which had broken with formal worship and preached a kind of universal brotherhood of men. Liszt attended some of their revivalist meetings and their philosophy made a lasting impact on him.

It was the July Revolution of 1830 which roused Liszt from his lethargy. He heard the sound of gunfire in the city, got up from his bed, and witnessed hand-to-hand fighting in the streets. These dramatic scenes acted like a catharsis on his pent-up emotions and brought him back to his senses. Those who saw him at this time testified to his completely changed appearance and enlivened looks; they took it to be a 'miracle cure'. Nowadays, with the benefit of our increased knowledge of psycho-therapy, it is not difficult to grasp the fact that Liszt was showing all the symptoms of severe depression, and that he was released from this condition by a series of powerful traumatic events. Anna put it quite tersely. 'The guns have cured him,' she said.

II

The Great Virtuoso

Paris in the 1830s was the centre of the pianistic world. Dozens of virtuosos played there including Kalkbrenner, Cramer, Moscheles, Dreyschock, Thalberg, Herz, Henselt and many others. They spent their lives, quite literally, crouched over a keyboard, bringing their fingers to an unbelievable state of perfection. Some of them even specialized in a particular branch of piano technique. There was Dreyschock with his octaves, Kalkbrenner with his passage-work, and Thalberg with his trick of making two hands sound like three. Dreyschock must have had wrists of steel, for he could play octaves as fast as other pianists played single notes. He used to stagger his audiences by performing Chopin's 'Revolutionary' Study with the difficult left hand part in octaves. And he produced an enormous sound. Heine used to say that when Dreyschock played his octaves in Munich, you could hear them in Paris when the wind was in the right direction. As for Kalkbrenner, the rapidity of his scale-work astonished everybody who heard it. Each note was crystal clear, each demi-semiquaver individually polished until it shone like a jewel. He was a machine-tooled pianist who functioned with perfect precision down to his last finger-joint. According to Paer, he directed his fingers like 'a well-drilled company of soldiers', and he would sit motionless before the keyboard as if he were a general behind the front lines following the progress of a battle. Henselt probably had the biggest hands in the business. His stretch was enormous. He eventually reached the point where he could take the notes B – E – A – C – E in his right hand alone, and in his left the notes C – E – G – C – F. But it cost him years of effort. He was rarely out of sight of a piano, and when he travelled he could be observed sitting in the corner of the stage-coach working out his fingerings at a dummy keyboard. He was a compulsive practiser and got into the bizarre habit of reading and talking while his robot hands worked away at a muffled piano as if guided by computer. He would meet people and hold conversations with them while carrying on his unremitting practice. He is said to have practised the entire set of forty-eight Preludes and Fugues while reading the Bible from cover to cover. This singular achievement endeared him to the hearts of the Russians at the Court at St. Petersburg, and he was rewarded with the title of Court Pianist. Then there was Thalberg. He was a master of the sustaining pedal and could send washes of colour across the hall. His big speciality was to bring out the melody with alternating thumbs in the middle of the keyboard, while surrounding it with cascades of arpeggios. It sounded as if he had three hands, and his audience used to lean forward in their seats to see how it was done. Thalberg was far more than a piano technician, however. At his best, he was an outstanding pianist who used the instrument as a genuine means of musical expression. I shall have more to say about Thalberg later, for he was the young Liszt's only serious rival; on one occasion he very nearly eclipsed him.

There was continual competition between these masters of the keyboard to gain popularity with the Paris audiences. Concert-goers watched with relish as one great pianist attempted to out-play another. Nowadays, we are amused by their circus-tricks. But this generation of pianists solved some of the most intractable problems of technique and raised the level of performance to unheard-of heights. Under their hands, the piano was transformed into one of the greatest musical instruments of the Romantic era.

Even as a young man Liszt was superior to them all. With his infallible technique he plunged into this musical turmoil of Paris and emerged the undisputed champion of the piano. And there, having reached the top of his profession, he might have stopped. He was nineteen years old.

In the lives of most great men there sometimes comes a moment when, in a blinding flash of revelation, they see their future destiny clearly mapped out before them. This happened to Liszt; and the 'blinding flash' occurred on the evening of 9 March 1831.

The foremost virtuoso of the age was not Liszt; it was the great violinist, Paganini. Already, during his own lifetime, Paganini had become a legend. His virtuosity was such that in order to account for it at all musicians supposed him to be in league with the Devil. Rumour had it that his fourth string, from which he could draw ravishing sounds, was made from the intestine of his wife whom he had murdered with his own hands. It was whispered that he had languished in jail for twenty years as a punishment for this crime, with a violin as his sole companion, and, being uniquely isolated from the outside world, he had thus wrested from the instrument its innermost secrets. There was no doubting his virtuosity. He created and solved his own technical problems. Everywhere, his works were regarded as unplayable. Paganini then turned up and played them. If a string broke, he could play equally well on three; if another broke, he could play equally well on two; in fact, his speciality was to play an entire piece on one string alone with which he would 'bring the house down'. Paganini guarded his secrets jealously. Whenever he rehearsed a concerto he would never allow the orchestral players a chance to observe what he did during the cadenza, for it was his habit to stop playing when this long-awaited moment arrived; with a nonchalent wave of the bow, he would indicate that the passage was to be taken 'as read'. Paganini played his cadenzas once, and once only, and that was at the public performance. Those were moments of supreme virtuosity, when the man and his violin became one, and the hushed audience would witness such marvels of execution that it seemed, indeed, as if the very Devil had taken possession of him.

It is easy to understand how the dark rumours about Paganini circulated when we consider his appearance. He dressed from head to foot in black. His body, racked with pain, was slowly wasting away from syphilis. He glided rather than walked across the stage—like a menacing vulture gently floating into position to consume its prey. His eyes had receded deep into their sockets and this, together with his waxen complexion, gave him a spectral appearance which was enhanced by the dark blue glasses he sometimes wore. The macabre impression was that of a bleached skull with a violin tucked under its chin.

On 9 March 1831 Paganini glided on to the stage of the Paris Opera House and played to a packed audience. The event had been eagerly awaited for weeks. This was Paganini's first visit to the city and people were agog to catch a glimpse of the living legend. Sitting in the audience that night was Liszt. He was electrified by Paganini's playing and the experience changed the course of his life. As he listened to the Italian wizard, he experienced what can only be described as a revelation. Here was a violinist who not only played his violin better than anyone else, but who had penetrated to the very core of its personality and unlocked its remaining potential. Paganini and the violin were indivisible. For some time, Liszt had intuitively known that he was destined to be more than a mere piano virtuoso, and it was Paganini who brought this truth home to him with renewed force. Henceforth he would make it his aim to play the piano not only better than anyone else, but to play it as well as it can be played—a very different proposition. He would become the Paganini of the piano.

Liszt now set himself a titanic programme of work. His practice sessions sometimes lasted fourteen hours a day. He wrote to a friend:

> For the past fortnight my mind and fingers have been working away like two lost souls. Homer, Châteaubriand, Beethoven, Bach, Hummel, Mozart, Weber, are all around me. I study them, meditate on them, devour them with fury; besides this, I practise four to five hours of exercises (3rds, 6ths, 8ves, tremolos, repetition of notes, cadenzas, etc.). Ah! provided I don't go mad, you will find in me an artist.

Four to five hours of exercises daily. It is a myth that Liszt never practised. His transcendental technique was achieved largely by sheer hard work.

Always, the ideal of Paganini was before him. His immediate aim was to create a new kind of repertoire for the piano in which he could transfer to the keyboard some of the more spectacular of Paganini's feats. To this end, he selected a group of Paganini's unaccompanied *Caprices*, notorious for their difficulties, and set about adapting their complex problems to the keyboard. He brought forth the first fruits of his labours in 1838, the *Six 'Paganini' Studies*, which represented a breakthrough in piano technique. The second of the set, the Study in E flat major, is typical of Liszt's achievement. Basically, Paganini's original piece is an exercise in scales and double-stops. The essence of the problem is how to switch effortlessly from the one technique to the other.

Liszt does far more than transfer these notes on to the keyboard. The results would hardly be piano music if he did. He transfers the problem as well, re-formulating it in pianistic terms.

Paganini Study no. 2, in E flat major

Left, Liszt in 1847; *right*, a portrait of Liszt aged twenty-eight by Jean Ingres

Liszt's three concert-platform rivals:

Above, Sigismond Thalberg; *below left*, Alexandre Dreyschock; *below right*,
Adolphe Henselt

How to jump from the last note of the scale to the chord immediately following? That is the problem. But it is not Liszt's problem; it is Paganini's. Liszt has simply built it into his transcription as faithfully as he can, thus retaining the essential technical point of Paganini's music. Later in the piece, Liszt introduces a variation on this passage in the form of double chromatic octaves, a device which Liszt actually invented and which is known to this day as 'Liszt octaves'.

Such passages sound colossal, and they sum up what it is that we mean when we talk about Liszt's 'transcendental' technique. The entire study is worth comparing with Paganini's original. It is a model of what the art of transcription should be.

Another of Liszt's 'Paganini' Studies is the famous *La Campanella*. It is based on an old Italian tune of the same name. Paganini played this tune everywhere and used to embellish it with brilliant variations, including some remarkable bell-like harmonics. He was so fond of the tune that he made it the main theme of the last movement of his Violin Concerto in B minor.

Ever since Érard had given Liszt a piano containing the 'double-escapement' action, which made rapid note-repetition easy, Liszt had been looking for an opportunity to explore the mechanism to the full. He found it in *Campanella*. The piece is a study in quick-fire note re-iteration such as the piano had never been challenged to play before.

The Great Virtuoso

Paganini Study no. 3: *La Campanella*

The other major group of piano pieces which Liszt completed at this time was his *Twelve Transcendental Studies*. They are even more difficult than the Paganini set. A fact which is not generally known about the *Transcendentals* is that they first started life in another form as young Liszt's Opus 1, a set of early keyboard studies which he composed when he was only fifteen years old. He now took these juvenile exercises and transformed them into works of towering difficulty. It is not clear why he chose to revise his 'prentice pieces, rather than to compose a completely fresh set. Perhaps the transformations came into being gradually, as a natural result of his improvising increasingly complex variations over the first models. This often happens, particularly with a composer who improvised as creatively as Liszt did. Whatever the explanation, it is illuminating to compare the two versions. Here, for example, is the opening of the Study in D minor, Opus 1, an exercise in double thirds, with alternating hands.

Compare it with what it later became: the great Transcendental Study No. 4: *Mazeppa*:

The double thirds are still there, but in a much more difficult form; moreover, they are now subservient to a new theme which strides across the keyboard with a giant's tread. At first glance, it almost seems as if three hands are needed to play it. No wonder Schumann described the *Transcendentals*, when he reviewed them in 1838, as 'studies in storm and dread, fit for only ten or twelve players in the world'. Liszt himself later came to regard their technical difficulties as so grave that he simplified them and published a new version in 1851, which is the one usually played today. This last version is the one to which he attached descriptive titles to most of the pieces; this does not mean he regarded them as 'programme music' however, for the titles were thought of long after the music was written.

Here are all the studies which Liszt completed during the 1830s under the direct influence of Paganini.

Six 'Paganini' Studies (completed 1838; revised 1851)

1.	G minor	4.	E major
2.	E flat major	5.	*La Chasse*
3.	*La Campanella*	6.	Theme and Variations

Twelve Transcendental Studies (completed 1838; revised and titled 1851)

1.	Prelude	7.	*Eroica*
2.	A minor	8.	*Wilde Jagd*
3.	*Paysage*	9.	*Ricordanza*
4.	*Mazeppa*	10.	F minor
5.	*Feux-follets*	11.	*Harmonies du soir*
6.	*Vision*	12.	*Chasse-neige*

Armed with this set of eighteen studies, which embodied every aspect of piano playing, Liszt now had a remarkable technical arsenal at his command, which clearly established his lead over all other pianists. Even today, few performers can play them all with equanimity.

While Liszt was living and working in Paris, creating a new brand of pianism, he made a number of important friends among the celebrated circle of artists then residing in the city, including Chopin, George Sand, Berlioz, Heine and Delacroix. It became the custom for them to meet for musical evenings which always finished up with Liszt playing until the small hours, with the others sitting round the piano spellbound. Even Chopin preferred to hear Liszt play his own (Chopin's) works rather than to play them himself, although later on he was to react against Liszt, both as a man and as a musician. One fateful evening the group assembled as usual, this time in Chopin's apartments. There, the twenty-two-year-old Liszt was introduced to the Countess Marie d'Agoult, the woman who was to dominate his life for the next six years. When Liszt first met her Marie was twenty-eight, unhappily married to a man considerably older than herself, and the mother of two young children. She was an extremely beautiful woman. Lina Ramann, Liszt's first biographer, described her as 'bewitchingly graceful, with a profusion of blonde hair that fell over her shoulders like a shower of gold'. Liszt was captivated by her. Marie, for her part, immediately fell under Liszt's spell.

In 1835 the pair eloped to Switzerland and the scandal rocked Paris. For better or worse, Liszt's fate was now sealed; for the rest of his life he was to be branded as a libertine, and vicious gossip would gather about him wherever he went. He and Marie settled in Geneva and there, from their sanctuary, they defied the world. At least they had no financial cares. The Countess came from a wealthy family of bankers and she had a considerable private income. This was supplemented by Liszt's salary from the Geneva Conservatoire whose Directors, after the initial shock of having the celebrated pianist descend on them in such unusual circumstances, were only too gratified to have him as a teacher. On 18 December, not long after their arrival in Geneva, their first child, Blandine, was born.

Whatever faults Liszt later came to find with Marie, for the time being she was a wholly beneficial influence on him. From the beginning she insisted that his true vocation was composing, and she created just the right domestic circumstances in which he could work. Although they were ostracized from Paris society for the moment, their friends rallied round. Geneva was not all that isolated, and a continuous stream of visitors descended on the couple at the Rue Tabazon where they lived. Throughout the spring and summer of 1836 there were frequent excursions into the idyllic Swiss countryside, and Liszt and his companions would sometimes ramble for miles under the hot sun, climbing hills and wading across mountain streams, returning home in the evenings utterly exhausted.

Among Liszt's compositions at this time were the ones which later formed the 'Swiss' volume of the great three-part collection of pieces called *Years of Pilgrimage*. They are distinctly impressionistic in character, and they reflect Liszt's feelings about the sights and sounds of Switzerland, whose great natural beauty enchanted him. The collection contains such 'atmospheric' pieces as *Orage* (A Storm), *Les Cloches de Genève* (The Bells of Geneva) and *Pastorale*. One of the more forward-looking items is *Au bord d'une source* (By a Spring), a piece of water-music prophetic of Ravel's *Jeux d'eau* in its evocation of splashing fountains.

Au bord d'une source

The Great Virtuoso

In September 1836 a picnic holiday was arranged at Chamonix, the party consisting of Liszt, Marie, George Sand and her friend Major Adolphe Pictet. The group also included three children: Blandine and George Sand's two children. Also accompanying them was Liszt's favourite pupil, Hermann Cohen, a youth who idolized Liszt and was inseparable from him. The assembled party must have presented a curious spectacle as they tramped through the Swiss countryside. Liszt's long, flowing hair was always the subject of comment, as was George Sand's male attire and her liking for cigars, while Major Pictet put the finishing touch to the picture with his colourful officer's uniform. They looked more like a band of strolling actors as they rambled along, arguing and gesticulating as they went. It was during this trip that Liszt revealed once again his extraordinary powers of improvisation. The party wandered into the little town of Fribourg and came across the church of St. Nicholas. There, Liszt saw a particularly fine organ built by the famous Mooser. He sat down and began to improvise a fantasia on the plainchant theme for the dead, *Dies Irae*, working up to a tremendous climax. Such was his involvement with the musical material that he continued extemporising for several hours and became oblivious to the presence of his companions. The episode made a lasting impression on the others. In later life, both Pictet and George Sand wrote about it.

Liszt had now been away from Paris for a year. During this time, under Marie's gentle influence, he had become a much more cultured person. They had read widely together, philosophy, literature, history, Marie's superior education spurring him to explore intellectual fields he had never before had the time or the inclination to enter. He had acquired a polish of mind and manner which remained with him for the rest of his life. It was an idyllic existence; yet Liszt became restless. He missed the social whirl of Paris. Above all, he wanted to return to the concert platform. It was two years since he had been heard in public and he had grown immeasurably in artistic stature since then; it was only natural that he should wish to flex himself before an audience again. But he had strong feelings of loyalty towards Marie that tied him to her; it was unthinkable to take her back to Paris; the scandal was too recent for that. Liszt might well have stayed at Geneva with Marie, and suppressed his rising ambitions, had it not been for the disturbing rumours which now started to come out of the French capital. A young Viennese pianist called Sigismond Thalberg had played there and created a sensation. People were openly comparing him with Liszt, who now had a perfect excuse for returning to Paris; his supremacy was threatened and it was essential that Thalberg should be conquered.

The Great Virtuoso

Sigismond Thalberg was born in 1812. He was the illegitimate son of Count Moritz von Dietrichstein and Baroness von Wetzler. It was his mother who had named him 'Thalberg'. After he was born she declared: 'May this child be a peaceful valley ('Thal'), but may he someday become a mountain ('Berg'). At first Thalberg was trained for a legal career, but he gave up law in order to devote himself fully to the piano. He was a pupil of Hummel's. He had a 'quiet' demeanour at the keyboard and he could produce a remarkably fine singing tone. Thalberg was renowned for his 'three-handed' effect which brought out the notes of a melody in the middle of the keyboard with alternating hands, the 'free' hand at any given moment providing an accompaniment of arpeggio-like figuration. The effect depended, to a large extent, on Thalberg's skilful use of the sustaining pedal to 'hold the line', so creating the magical illusion of a third hand.

Liszt first heard Thalberg in March 1837 at the Paris Conservatoire. On the programme were two of Thalberg's war-horses: the Fantasia on *God Save the Queen* and the Fantasia on Rossini's opera *Moses*. Long before the programme was finished Liszt knew that he need have no fears. Thalberg was a pianist of considerable talent, but he was not a genius. As for the vaunted three-handed effect, it was a clever trick, no more. Liszt now planned his campaign carefully. The first step was to bring Thalberg out fighting. An opportunity quickly presented itself. When asked what he thought of Thalberg, Liszt replied: 'He is the only man I know who plays the violin on the piano.' The remark set the whole of Paris laughing. Thalberg was considerably put out. When he was asked to make a joint appearance with Liszt, he retaliated: 'I do not like to be accompanied.' It was Liszt's turn to be offended. He proceeded to rent the Paris Opera House to give a recital, an unprecedented thing to do in those days as its auditorium held about 4,000 people—more than ten times the number Thalberg had played to in the Conservatoire. The snub was pointed. In the face of such mounting provocation Thalberg could not ignore Liszt and an open trial of strength between the two pianists was inevitable.

The spectacle presented itself on 31 March 1837 in the salon of the Princess Belgiojoso, one of the most colourful personalities in Paris society. She was famous for her charity concerts. Shrewdly observing the mounting tension between Liszt and his rival, she was quick to seize the advantage. She invited both pianists to appear at her *salon*, together with other artists, in aid of the Italian refugees. Everybody in Paris knew that this was simply a superb piece of diplomatic bluff designed to bring the two men face to face; the Princess had scored the social *coup* of the season.

The following advertisement appeared in the *Gazette Musicale* on 26 March.

> The greatest interest . . . will be without question the simultaneous appearance of two talents whose rivalry at this time agitates the musical world, and is like the indecisive balance between Rome and Carthage. MM. Listz [*sic*] and Thalberg will take turns at the piano.

So fierce was the demand to see Liszt and Thalberg 'take turns' that the Princess was able to charge 40 francs a ticket. Thalberg played first, giving another performance of his *Moses* Fantasia. Then Liszt appeared and played his *Niobe* Fantasia, a new piece he had just completed, full of glittering technical devices which showed him off to best advantage. Liszt received the ovation of the evening and all doubts about his supremacy were dispelled. As for Thalberg, his humiliation was complete. He virtually disappeared from the concert platform after this date. Eventually, he retired to a small Italian village near Naples where he apparently bought a vineyard and ended his days cultivating grapes.

After his victory over Thalberg, Liszt was content to retire once again from the concert platform—for the time being, at any rate. He left Paris and travelled to Nohant to stay with George Sand at her country home. Marie rejoined him there. They had been apart for several weeks. If there had been one or two differences between Liszt and Marie before he left Geneva, they were now forgotten in the joy of reunion and the two lovers started to make ambitious plans to tour the Italian lakes, an idea that had long been in their minds. They left Nohant in July 1837, making their way first to Lyons. A few weeks later, they had crossed the border into Italy.

This was the first time either of them had visited Italy, and they soon succumbed to its wonderful atmosphere. They lingered for days by the shores of Lake Maggiore, and then they moved on to the tiny village of Bellagio which was lapped by the warm waters of Lake Como and which so enchanted them that they rented the Villa Medici there in order to prolong their stay. Here they read Dante and Petrarch together, two poets who had a profound effect on Liszt's creative development. They also made excursions into various towns in northern Italy, touring the art galleries and contemplating the great sculptures and paintings of the Renaissance. On Christmas Eve, 1837, the event for which they had prolonged their stay at Bellagio took place, and Marie gave birth to another daughter. She was named Cosima, after Lake Como.

Liszt reacted to the stimulating environment of Italy by a fresh flowering

The Great Virtuoso

Il Penseroso

of his creative faculties, and he now started work on the second, 'Italian' volume of the *Years of Pilgrimage*. Unlike the earlier 'Swiss' volume, whose pieces are impressionistic nature pictures, the ones in the 'Italian' volume are mostly inspired by existing works of art, as their titles show. The first is called *Sposalizio* (The Wedding) after Raphael's painting of that name; while the second is named *Il Penseroso* (The Thinker) after Michelangelo's famous sculpture. These two pieces are unaccountably neglected in recitals

Sonetto 104 del Petrarca

today. *Il Penseroso* is a remarkable achievement harmonically and is far in advance of its time (see page 41).

Also to be found in the 'Italian' volume, although composed a few years later, are the three Petrarch Sonnets. They were originally composed as songs, but they are better known in their solo piano version. The second one, *Sonetto 104 del Petrarca* is the most frequently played of the group and it has become justly famous. The most significant work in the collection is the 'Dante' Sonata, one of Liszt's masterpieces. Its full title is *Après une lecture du Dante: Fantasia quasi Sonata*. Liszt completed it in the space of a few weeks by the shores of Lake Como, shortly before Christmas 1837. It reflects his readings of Dante's *Inferno* and tries to portray in music the 'strange tongues, horrible cries, words of pain and tones of anger' Dante described in his descent to Hell. The work begins with a declamatory introduction based, appropriately, on the tritone—*Diabolus in Musica*. It is as if the gates of Hell were swinging open.

'Dante' Sonata

The first subject depicts the souls of Hell moaning in anguish. Its wailing, tortured chromaticism is a stroke of great originality.

Liszt's pedal marks have been the subject of much comment. Some pianists think that if you play exactly what Liszt wrote (see page 42) the passage is blurred. This is perfectly true. But even on the lighter pianos of his day it sounds no clearer. We must assume, then, that the distant, ominous roar is what Liszt wanted. His pedal effects are, as a rule, meticulous and, as in this case, often daring.

A choral-like theme, which forms the second subject, now rises out of the flames of Hell. It is heard in two versions; first, in a great passionate outburst, (see page 44) and again, almost immediately afterwards, in an atmosphere of utter calm.

These two versions of the second subject theme should be closely compared. They contain the germ of a variation technique known as the 'transformation of themes' which Liszt was to develop exhaustively in later life. In the 'Dante' Sonata, the young Liszt was still feeling his way towards this technique. If you look at the Coda, you will discover that the second subject

Presto agitato assai

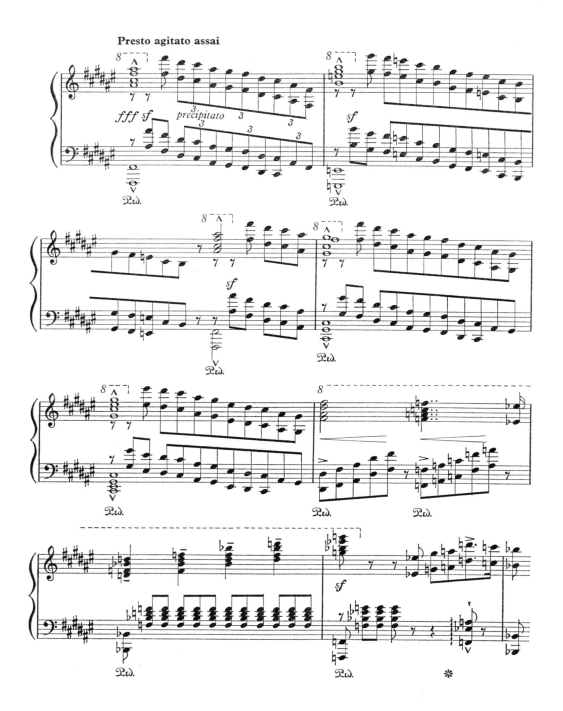

theme turns up yet again, this time to suggest the scene where Dante gazes up towards Heaven and hears in the distance the music of Paradise.

The 'Dante' Sonata raises in a particularly acute form the whole question of 'programme' music, and how far (if at all) a literary work of art, or any other work of art, can be expressed through music. Liszt himself took many years to formulate his views about the subject. They are discussed on p. 59.

In April 1838 Liszt read in the newspapers of the disastrous flooding of the Danube, and the havoc it had created in his native Hungary. The misfortune which had descended on his own people, many of whom were starving, galvanized Liszt into action and he left Italy for Vienna to give concerts in aid of the victims. He had not been heard there since he was a boy. Ten concerts were arranged and they were completely sold out, raising more than £2,000 for the relief of the sufferers. These Austrian concerts represented a distinct turning-point in Liszt's life. The tremendous response he received from the public confirmed for him, once and for all, what he had inwardly felt for a long time: that he was not only miraculously endowed as a pianist, but that his commanding stage-presence enabled him to mesmerize his audiences, and even generate hysteria in them. Clara Schumann, not the most generous of critics, was bowled over.

> We have heard Liszt. He can be compared to no other virtuoso. He is the only one of his kind. He arouses fright and astonishment. . . . His attitude at the piano cannot be described. He is original; he grows sombre at the piano. His passion knows no limits.

There were irresistible powers stirring within Liszt that were to give him no rest. From this time, he was to feel increasingly the pull of the concert platform. Meanwhile, there were Marie and the children to consider. He could not abandon them. Nor had he any wish to do so at present, although the first sign of strain revealed itself in his relations with Marie just now. He returned to Italy, resolved to resume their idyllic life together.

The couple spent the summer of 1838 in Lugano, and towards the end o the year they moved to Rome. Here Liszt became friendly with the famous painter Ingres, who was then the Director of the French Academy in the Villa Medici and a keen amateur violinist. Ingres used to discuss with Liszt the many works of art under his care, and in the evenings Liszt often returned the gesture by playing for him. The famous drawing of Liszt by Ingres dates from this period (see facing p. 32). Liszt's third child, a son called Daniel, was born during their stay in Rome. Marie had now three children to cope with, and Liszt began to find her temper irksome. They quarrelled frequently and gradually became disillusioned in one another.

It now needed only one event of any significance to trigger off an explosion between them, and it duly presented itself. They had left Rome in June 1839 to escape the summer heat and travelled to the seaside village of San Rossore *via* Pisa. It was here that Liszt heard news which was to change the course of his career. The Beethoven Memorial Committee in Bonn announced that their international scheme to raise funds for a Beethoven Monument at the place of his birth had collapsed through lack of support. The French section had disgraced itself by producing the paltry sum of 424 francs 90 centimes (about £25 or $70). Liszt was angered by this insult to Beethoven whom he had idolized since his youth. Rather than see the scheme collapse he now offered to take it on single-handed. He wrote first to the sculptor Bartolini of Florence, to discover the cost of a statue in marble. He then set out his terms to the Memorial Committee in the following manner.

Gentlemen,

As the subscription for the Beethoven Monument is only getting on slowly, and as the carrying out of this undertaking seems rather far distant, I venture to make a proposal to you, the acceptance of which would make me very happy.

I offer myself to make up, from my own means, the sum still wanting for the erection of the monument, and ask no further privilege than that of naming the artist who shall execute the work. That artist is Bartolini of Florence, who is universally considered the first sculptor in Italy.

I have spoken to him about the matter provisionally, and he assures me that a monument in marble (which would cost about 50 to 60 thousand francs) could be finished in two years, and he is ready to begin the work at once.

I have the honour to be, etc.,

FRANZ LISZT

Pisa, Oct. 3rd, 1839

It was now inevitable that Liszt should return to the concert platform; this was the only way he could raise the money. Marie grieved over his decision; she genuinely believed it to be against his best interests as a composer. Moreover, she feared that it might drive a permanent wedge between them; a family of three was a liability and Liszt could not possibly take them with him on his travels. By the autumn of 1839 Liszt had announced his opening concerts, and the Countess d'Agoult, deeply embittered, returned to Paris with her family. 'Franz had abandoned me,' she later wrote, 'for such small motives.'

Liszt has often been blamed for his seemingly callous attitude towards Marie; but whatever pain and humiliation he caused her (and he caused her both) it was vindicated by his subsequent pianistic career which has remained unmatched in the history of performance. He virtually created the solo piano recital; indeed, the very term 'recital' was his. He was the first to establish the practice, followed to this day, of playing his programmes from memory; the first to range across the entire piano repertory, as it then existed, from Bach to Chopin; the first to tour Europe from the Pyrenees to the Urals; the first to raise the level of solo performances from circus stunts to valid artistic experiences.

The eight years between 1839 and 1847 are sometimes called Liszt's years of transcendental execution. It is not often realized that his legendary fame as a pianist, which he continued to enjoy long after he had retired from the concert platform for good, rested mainly on his spectacular achievements during this relatively short period. The stories about him abound. On one occasion Liszt visited St. Petersburg and was confronted by the court pianist Dreyschock playing (inevitably) Chopin's 'Revolutionary' Study with the left hand thundering away in octaves. Liszt was asked what he thought of this feat. His 'reply' was to play Chopin's F minor Study (Opus 25, no. 2) with the rapid right hand triplets in a delicate whisper; on reaching the final C's in the right hand he opened it wide to take the octave and repeated

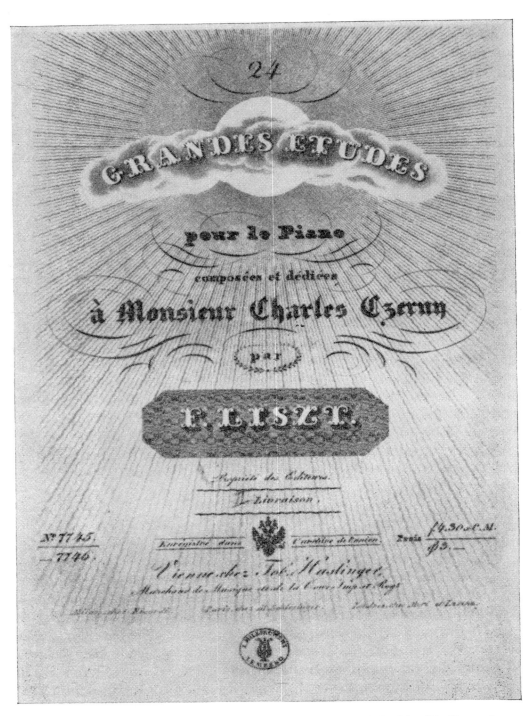

The second version of the Transcendental Studies published by Haslinger in 1839

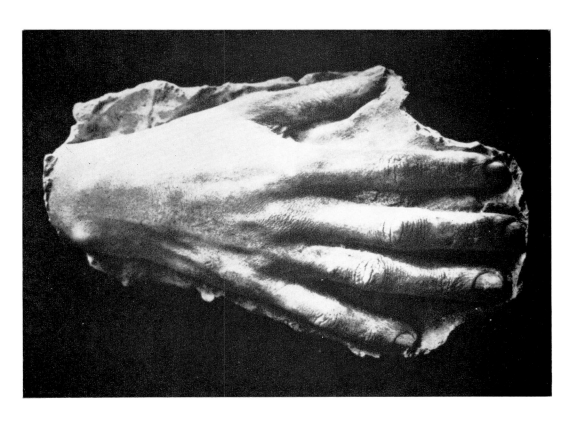

Above, a plaster cast of Liszt's right hand

Below, the Sword of Honour presented to the composer in Budapest, 1840

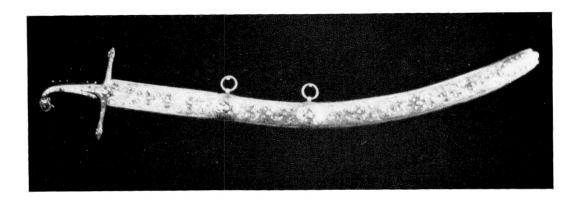

Above, a contemporary caricature of Liszt receiving the Sword of Honour

Below, the Altenburg, Weimar

the whole Study *fortissimo*, *à la* Dreyschock in a whirl of octaves. The point was obvious: Liszt could play both ways. Moreover, his musical skills matched his technical ones. On another occasion Liszt was playing in Dublin and, following his usual custom, he asked the audience to submit themes on which he might improvise. Three themes were eventually handed in. Much to the audience's pleasure, he improvised variations on each theme in turn; then—a typically Lisztian touch, this—as the applause was dying down he sat down once more and brought the whole thing to a remarkable climax by combining all three themes in the most ingenious manner. He was weighed down with medals and decorations from different countries, some of which he wore on stage, including the bejewelled sword of honour presented to him by his fellow Hungarians. It prompted some bright wit to pen these lines:

> Liszt alone, of all warriors, is without reproach.
> For despite his big sword, we know that this
> Has vanquished only semiquavers
> And slain only pianos.

There may have been some justice in the criticism. Liszt quite frequently slew his pianos. The instruments of his day were often little better than boxes of wood and wire. Lacking the modern iron frame, they were totally unable to withstand the onslaught of his bigger works and he sometimes left a trail of broken debris behind him. It became his custom never to walk on to the platform unless there was a reserve piano ready to be pushed into position at a moment's notice. As for his decorations, Liszt wore them not merely through vanity, but to raise the status of musicians everywhere who were all too often regarded as a lower species. Here, he seemed to say, was one musician at least who had as many titles as a prince. It was a gesture of defiance. It falls into the same category as his classic reply to Tsar Nicholas I who started talking during one of Liszt's recitals. Liszt stopped playing and sat at the keyboard with bowed head. When Nicholas enquired the cause of the hushed silence, Liszt replied: 'Music herself should be silent when Nicholas speaks.' The remark probably cost Liszt a medal.

Liszt announced that his opening concerts would take place in Vienna. They were sold out days in advance. Three thousand people were present at his first recital, including the Dowager Empress. The success of the Beethoven Monument was assured. Six concerts had been advertised but he was forced to give ten. In an amusing letter to Marie, Liszt observes that he had become so famous that even the doctor treating him for his cold—

he had arrived in Vienna with influenza—had suddenly become inundated with new patients requesting not treatment, but news of the great pianist!

While Liszt was in Vienna, a deputation of Hungarians called on him with an invitation to visit his native land. He had not been to Hungary since he was a child; now, eighteen years later, he was the most celebrated Hungarian alive, and his people wished to acknowledge the fact. Revolution was in the air. They were shortly to spill their blood in an attempt to gain independence. Meanwhile, Liszt had become something of a national symbol. He set out for Budapest arriving there on Christmas Eve, 1839. People lined the streets as he passed by in his coach with Count Esterházy at his side, and Barons Benckheim and Zichy a short distance behind—three of the most important magnates in Hungary. Liszt gave a series of recitals in Budapest, and then paid a nostalgic visit to his native village of Raiding and saw again the cottage where he was born. He was serenaded by the local

Hungarian Rhapsody no. 11, in A minor

gipsies, whose music he tried to capture in his Hungarian Rhapsodies, the first of which he began to write about this time. The cimbalom effect—that most characteristic of gipsy musical sounds—turns up frequently and lends the Rhapsodies a curiously authentic personality (see page 50).

It was during this visit that Liszt was presented with his jewel-encrusted sword of honour, and there are pictures of him at this time resplendent in national Hungarian costume.

If his stay in Hungary was a triumph (and it is all faithfully detailed in his letters to Marie) his reception in Berlin in 1842 can only be described as hysterical. The adulation of the public reached ludicrous proportions. The emotionally charged atmosphere of his recitals made them more like séances than serious musical events. In two months, he gave twenty-one concerts in Berlin and played more than eighty works, most of them from memory, an indication of his enormous repertoire. The **King of Prussia,** **Frederick-William IV,** was present at most of them. He presented Liszt with a valuable purse of diamonds, but Liszt contemptuously threw it into the wings—another of his 'gestures'—an act of courage which endeared him to the hearts of everybody in the audience, for the Prussian monarch was not popular.

'Franz Liszt in Berlin', 1842

Liszt had now perfected one of his most telling *genres* of composition, the Operatic Paraphrase, which usually took the form of a brilliant show-piece based on themes from the well-known operas of the day, and which never failed to make an impact. One of the most effective is the *Réminiscences de Norma* (1841) after Bellini's opera. Busoni once said of the magical middle section *Qual cor tradisti,* that anyone who listens to it without being moved has not yet arrived at Liszt.

51

Reminiscences of Bellini's *Norma* ('Qual cor tradisti')

The Operatic Paraphrase has fallen out of fashion since Liszt's day, mainly because of the 'purists' who dislike the notion of one composer tampering with the work of another. But practically all the great composers have indulged in the art of arrangement, which usually calls for considerable skill, and there is a strong indication that pianists are re-discovering Liszt's contributions to this field and valuing them as works of art in their own right—which, in a sense, is what they are.

When Liszt finally left Berlin he was driven to the Brandenburg gate in a splendid coach driven by six white horses; thirty other carriages followed behind in procession. It was preposterous; it was as though a reigning monarch were taking leave of his people.

Together with his musical conquests went his romantic ones. Liszt's career as a Don Juan has never been fully chronicled, but by any standards it was extraordinary. Women found him irresistible. With his mesmeric personality, his good looks, and his Byronic manner, he swept all before him. Few of his encounters with the opposite sex were anything more than passing affairs. But they did his reputation harm. One or two created a scandal, particularly the Lola Montez episode, which he never succeeded in living down. Lola Montez was a dancer who achieved notoriety by once baring her ample breasts on stage before Ludwig I of Bavaria. When Liszt first met her she was twenty-three. He quickly tired of her, but unlike the others, Lola was not to be jilted so easily. Liszt tried to make his escape by bribing the hotel porter to lock her in their hotel room while he fled to another town. But Lola had the temper of a tigress and planned revenge. She pursued Liszt, much to his embarrassment. The climax of the scandal came when Liszt attended the dinner given in his honour at Bonn for the unveiling of the Beethoven Monument. Lola Montez burst in, jumped on the table, and executed one of her dances before the astonished guests. It was scandals such as these which put the finishing touch to Liszt's break with the Countess d'Agoult. Liszt and Marie had made an attempt to patch up their differences by spending the summers of 1841 and 1842 at Nonnenwerth, an island on the Rhine, which Liszt had rented for the holidays. But Marie was increasingly mortified by the notoriety which surrounded Liszt; whatever he did became the subject of instant gossip which, for a woman in her position, was intolerable. As she herself put it, she did not mind being his mistress; but she refused to be *one* of his mistresses. The Lola Montez affair was the last straw. After 1845 Marie and Liszt broke off all contact with one another.

Liszt now extended his tours to include Spain, Portugal, Turkey and even Russia which, in those days, was a closed continent. These were triumphal years for him. But in retrospect, we can see that they laid the foundations for many of the hostile criticisms which were to stain his reputation among certain members of the musical profession. Sober-minded musicians like Mendelssohn, Schumann and Chopin were alienated by his victories. They saw something in his personality—the actor, the showman, the trickster, even—which they abhorred. Time and again, Liszt was accused of 'playing to the gallery', and there may have been some truth in the charge even though it is oversimplified. If we wish to understand Liszt's musical personality during these years, one man, and one man alone, holds the key: Paganini. Paganini was a torch by whose light Liszt found his way. There is the same emphasis on dazzling virtuosity, the same skill in whipping up hysteria, the same touch of the macabre and the diabolical. Liszt's art and Paganini's are welded indissolubly together. The awe and reverence Liszt felt for the Italian master's 'black art' came out strongly at the time of Paganini's death in 1840, the circumstances of which make horrific reading even today. The Church considered him an atheist, and withheld the last rites; worse, they refused to allow his corpse to be buried on consecrated ground. A long and bitter dispute began between Paganini's friends and the Clergy. Meanwhile, the body, which had been embalmed, remained unburied. Crowds of sightseers milled outside the house, crossing themselves, trying to catch a glimpse of the unshriven corpse which lay on a makeshift platform, its glassy eyes opened wide. A large bandage held its sagging jaw in position, and a nightcap was perched on its head at a bizarre angle. It was soon considered expedient to place it in a temporary coffin with a glass pane covering the face. One of Paganini's aristocratic friends, the Count de Cessole, was appalled at the Church's attitude, and offered to have the body buried on his estates. It was carried by night along the peninsula of St. Jean-Cap-Ferrat on to his property at Cap Sainte-Hospice where it remained for several years. During the next two decades, Paganini was exhumed and reburied several times. Finally, after more than forty years of wrangling, the coffin was lowered into a permanent resting-place at Parma with the full approval of the Vatican, and it remains there to this day. The coffin was opened at least twice after this at the behest of people fascinated by the Paganini legend, the last time being in 1896.

The one civilized voice to be raised in Paganini's defence was Liszt's. He felt such a deep sense of personal loss when the great violinist died that he published an obituary notice of him. Amidst all the superstitious nonsense surrounding Paganini, and the gruesome details of his death which were published in every newspaper in Europe and swallowed hungrily by a sensation-seeking public, Liszt's compassionate article stands out as a magnificent tribute from one great artist to another. The article is a long one, but the following quotation is typical of its general tone.

> The flame of Paganini's life is extinguished; with him vanished one of those wonders which Nature seems to bestow upon us only to reclaim it as hastily as possible—a miracle which the kingdom of art has seen but once.
>
> None will succeed him, none may be called his equal in fame. His name will never be mentioned in connection with another. For what artist's fame has enjoyed such unclouded sunlight; who is his equal in the enthusiastic and undivided opinion of the world as the ruler in the kingdom of art?

Paganini was dead. But his shade lived on in Liszt.

III

At Weimar

In 1847 Liszt took a momentous decision. He turned his back on the piano and retired from the concert platform for good. The last recital he ever gave for money was in Elizabetgrad during a tour of the Ukraine. He was thirty-five years old.

The idea had long been germinating in his mind. The life of a travelling virtuoso had become increasingly irksome to him. He wanted leisure to compose. As early as 1842 he had been invited to take up the position of Kapellmeister to the court at Weimar. The thought of taking up residence there held many attractions for him. Weimar was one of the most cultured cities in Germany. It throve under the benign patronage of the Grand Duchess Marie-Pavlovna of Saxe-Weimar, sister of Tsar Nicholas I of Russia. Already, it could boast more than a century's unbroken association with the arts. Bach had lived and worked there; so, too, had Goethe and Schiller. Moreover, Weimar possessed a good orchestra and an opera-house. It was an attractive offer, and Liszt now decided to accept it.

It was during this last tour of the Ukraine that Liszt encountered the woman who was to become the second great love of his life, the Princess Carolyne Sayn-Wittgenstein. He was giving charity concerts in Kiev and the Princess was in the audience. Afterwards she sent a handsome donation to him, and it was in the course of thanking her that a personal meeting took place. Carolyne was twenty-eight, seven years younger than Liszt. She was already separated from her husband, Prince Nicholas Sayn-Wittgenstein, whom she had married while still a girl of seventeen, and she had a small daughter. Polish by birth, she was an extremely wealthy woman in her own right, holding vast estates in the Ukraine and exercising total dominion over some 30,000 serfs. She is described as having clear blue eyes, a pale complexion, and blonde hair. In addition to these attributes, she displayed a passion for cigars. She was not a particularly beautiful woman, but she had great force of character. Within weeks of their first meeting, the Princess had thrown in her lot with Liszt's and resolved to follow him to Weimar. On the face of it, this was a reckless plan. There seemed to be nothing to distinguish Carolyne from all the other colourful conquests Liszt had made in recent years. She appeared totally unsuitable as a permanent partner. But this is to disregard Liszt's state of mind at this time. He longed for domestic tranquillity. We know he was contemplating marriage. In 1845 he had gone so far as to propose to the Countess Valentine Cessiat, the niece of Lamartine, who in turn had gone so far as to turn him down. There seems little doubt that both Liszt and the Princess believed an annulment of her marriage was imminent and that in a short time she would be free to re-marry. Unfortunately, this was not to be. Although they lived together in Weimar for the next twelve years, the marriage never took place owing to the joint machinations of the Tsarist court and the Vatican. Meantime, Carolyne was to be a powerful influence on Liszt, and she became increasingly involved in his creative development. Liszt's biographers have been unnecessarily harsh on her. She has been variously depicted as an intellectual blue-stocking, a religious bigot, and an incessant meddler in Liszt's affairs. But it must be remembered that Carolyne met a genuine need on Liszt's part. She was receptive to his ideas, sympathetic to his aims, and she invariably placed his artistic interests before her own. Moreover, she was to provide Liszt with a comfortable home for several years, at a crucial time in his life, when he took immense strides forward in the field of composition. It is doubtful that he could have achieved so much without her help and encouragement. It was at Weimar that Liszt composed his great B minor Piano Sonata, and the 'Faust' and 'Dante' Symphonies, arguably his three finest masterpieces. In addition, he also composed there his unique series of 12 Symphonic Poems—a form he invented—which was to have untold historical consequences. He developed the orchestra at Weimar to such a pitch of excellence that it came to be reckoned one of the best in Europe. He initiated a steady stream of productions from the opera-house, giving the first performance of several operas, including Wagner's *Lohengrin* and Schumann's *Genoveva*. Pupils flocked to him from the four quarters, and his master-classes in piano-playing became world-famous. All in all, then, Carolyne was far from being the malignant influence that history depicts. This groundless charge is denied by the evidence of Liszt's creative output during these years.

Carolyne arrived at Weimar in July 1848 and took up residence at the Altenburg, the house which Liszt was to make famous throughout the musical world. The Altenburg stands in Weimar to this day. It is not a par-

A caricature of Liszt in 1847

ticularly distinguished house, but its rooms are spacious and it offered a comfortable home for Liszt and the Princess. Liszt took over one small wing of the house as his own personal quarters, consisting of a bedroom with a linking door to his study, and it was here that he did most of his composing. These rooms were modestly furnished, the largest item being a Bechstein grand piano of which he was particularly fond. There were only two pictures on the walls: an engraving of Dürer's 'Melancholia' and an artist's impression of 'St. Francis walking on the waters' which later inspired his piano composition of the same name. By contrast, the rest of the house, which he shared with the Princess, was a treasure-trove full of items he had collected on his tours—including Beethoven's Broadwood piano and the priceless death-mask of Beethoven—much of which he had stored with his mother in Paris until a permanent place could be found for it all. The domestic routine was simple. Liszt rose early in the morning and composed until midday; during the afternoons he sometimes took a piano class; in the evenings, he and the Princess would hold open house and receive guests. An evening in the Altenburg was one to be cherished in the memory.

Liszt's intention was to place Weimar in the vanguard of modern music. Vienna, which had dominated the scene for sixty years, had lapsed into arid academicism since the death of Beethoven. The position in Leipzig was even worse; Mendelssohn had been cut off in his prime and the schoolmen had taken over, the 'little Leipzigers' Hauptmann, Rietz and Ferdinand David, who placed modern music in a straitjacket. As for Paris, it was dominated by the Opera House and it was virtually impossible for an unknown composer to gain a foothold there. The younger generation of composers now looked to Weimar and Liszt for leadership, and it was quickly forthcoming. With characteristic generosity, he placed himself and his resources wholeheartedly at the service of all who sought his help. No cause, however unworthy, was turned away, even where his own preferences failed to correspond to it. Overnight, Weimar became the Mecca of modern music, and a steady stream of visitors converged on the city—Wagner, Brahms and Berlioz among them.

Historians still refer to that band of disciples who grouped themselves around Liszt in the 1850s as the 'Neo-German' School. What was the 'Neo-German' School? What did it stand for, and what were its achievements?

Liszt's philosophy of music is seriously misunderstood, even today. This is curious, as he went to great trouble to express himself clearly and precisely.

The central problem agitating the world of music in the 1850s was the fate of sonata form. There were only two alternatives open to composers: either they could go on repeating the formula handed down to them by the Viennese classics, or they could attempt to modify and develop it. Broadly speaking, Mendelssohn and Brahms chose the former alternatives; Liszt chose the latter. His work shows three distinct departures.

(1) He evolved the single-movement 'cyclic' sonata structure which rolled the separate movements into one, and had its final outcome in the symphonic poem. In this, Liszt was carrying on a procedure hinted at by Beethoven in whose later works—the Fifth Symphony, for example—certain movements are linked together.

(2) He perfected the 'transformation of themes' technique in which the contrasting ideas of a work are all developed out of a single theme. A simple illustration occurs in the A major Piano Concerto which Liszt completed at Weimar. Its lyrical, opening theme

Piano Concerto no. 2, in A major

is later transformed into the march-tune of the finale.

This tune, in turn, is transformed into the following, impassioned theme which appears near the end of the Concerto.

The 'transformation of themes' technique is essentially that of variation. A basic idea undergoes constant development, appearing in several different disguises. This kind of procedure placed the whole question of structural 'integrity' into a new context which was to have repercussions right down to our own time. Beethoven again pointed the way in the Fifth Symphony where the main theme of the Scherzo recurs in a 'transformation' in the middle of the finale.

(3) Liszt believed that the language of music could be fertilized by the other arts, poetry and painting in particular. He popularized the concept of 'programme' music and so began a controversy which goes on to this day. No other article of Liszt's musical faith has been so badly misrepresented as this one. There are still musicians who think that Liszt fostered the absurd notion that music is a 'representative' art, that it can 'depict' a poem, a picture, a flower or a storm. Of course, it does no such thing, and Liszt never said that it could. He is quite plain on the matter.

> It is obvious that things which can appear only objectively to perception can in no way furnish connecting points to music; the poorest of apprentice landscape painters could give with a few chalk strokes a much more faithful picture than a musician operating with all the resources of the best orchestra. But if these same things are subjectivated to dreaming, to contemplation, to emotional uplift, have they not a peculiar kinship with music; and should not music be able to translate them into its mysterious language?

In other words, music cannot 'depict' a poem, a picture, a flower or a storm. What it does is far more subtle. It expresses the 'mood' that such a poem or picture evokes, and transmutes it into a musical experience, an experience to be perceived on a purely musical level. It was in this spirit that Liszt composed his symphonic poems; it is in this spirit that we should hear them. Their titles—'Hamlet', 'Tasso', 'Les Préludes', 'Orpheus'—are simply a disclosure of the *source* of Liszt's inspiration, not a clue to some story hidden in the music. As to the literary programmes with which Liszt adorned these scores, they were invariably placed there *after* the music was composed. Sometimes, they were not even written by Liszt; one or two, we know, were written by the Princess Wittgenstein who had literary pretensions. This fact alone should dispel the legend that the music is 'about' something, in the crude sense, and bring back Liszt into the fold of 'absolute' composers. For the rest, his attitude towards programme music was derived from Beethoven, the Beethoven of the 'Pastorale' Symphony. And if questioned about it, Liszt might well have replied with Beethoven that his music, like the 'Pastorale', was more the 'expression of feeling than painting'.

This, briefly, was the philosophical position of the 'Neo-German' School. Liszt was to have many followers, and the symphonic poem which embodied his ideas was taken up by such composers as Richard Strauss, in a sense Liszt's true heir, and Sibelius.

Until he arrived in Weimar, Liszt had little chance to get to grips with the orchestra. Practically all his compositions before 1848 had been for piano solo. True, one or two involved the orchestra, like the 'Lélio' Fantasy, but they revealed an amateurish approach to the problems of instrumentation and Liszt now resolved to master this field once and for all. It says much for his artistic integrity that he was not above asking for help and advice from Conradi and Joachim Raff, his professional assistants during his early days at Weimar. But there is no sense in which the orchestral pieces are not entirely Liszt's own work; he continually revised them in the light of his rapidly increasing knowledge of the orchestra, and the final versions do not contain a note he did not pen. After 1854 Liszt dispensed with Raff completely (Conradi had left Weimar as early as 1849) and thereafter he undertook all his orchestrating himself. Just how far Liszt advanced in this direction may be seen in the symphonic poem *Orpheus*, which he composed in 1854. This piece is a little gem which is full of the most felicitous touches of colour. The opening pages, in which we hear Orpheus strumming his lute, are particularly effective.

The work which best sums up Liszt's achievement at Weimar is the Sonata in B minor which he completed in 1853. It represents one of the most successful solutions to the problem of sonata form to come out of the nineteenth century. The Sonata, which unfolds nearly half-an-hour's unbroken music, is really an immense 'first movement' form; not only are the four contrasting movements here rolled into one, but they are themselves composed against a background of a full-scale sonata scheme—Exposition,

The Faust Symphony published in 1861 and dedicated to Berlioz

Development and Recapitulation—in a masterly and brilliant *tour de force*. Nowhere is the 'transformation of themes' technique seen to better advantage. The entire structure is generated from a tiny group of thematic 'tags' which are first heard in the Introduction. See brackets 'X', 'Y' and 'Z'.

Piano Sonata in B minor

Liszt now goes on to derive his first subject from a skilful combination of 'Y' and 'Z'. Compare it with the previous example.

The second subject is derived in a similar way. Its gentle, flowing lyricism appears to place it a long way from anything previously heard in the Sonata; but on closer inspection we recognize 'Z' in augmentation.

The Development section contains an ingenious three-part fugue, whose main subject sounds like a mocking parody of the earlier ideas 'Y' and 'Z' (see page 65).
At one point, the fugue subject is turned upside down.

Very few sonatas in the nineteenth century attempted to combine fugal technique with sonata form, and none (with the exception of Beethoven's) does it more successfully. Throughout the Sonata Liszt rings the changes on his basic material in this fashion. Even the dreaded double-octave passage, in the Coda, turns out to be a variation on 'Y'.

The Sonata is too long and complex to be properly analysed here. But it is a key work in Liszt's output, and no student of Liszt can afford to overlook it. Sometimes, one hears the work explained in terms of a 'programme'. Liszt is supposed to have had Goethe's *Faust* in mind when he wrote it, the first subject depicting Faust, the second subject portraying Gretchen, and Mephistopheles being represented by the fugue. It is even maintained that the work is autobiographical in character and that its conflicts spring from the contradictions in Liszt's own personality. Needless to say, no such interpretation was ever sanctioned by Liszt himself. The widespread

The composer aged fifty-two, a portrait by M. Stein

An oil portrait of Liszt in 1857 by W. von Kaulbach

Above, the Music Room at the Hofgärtnerei

Below, Liszt on his death-bed at Bayreuth, 1886

Allegro energico

E

tradition of seeing the work in this colourful light seems to have started with Liszt's biographer Peter Raabe.

With so much positive achievement behind him, why did Liszt come to regard his years at Weimar as a bitter failure? What were the circumstances which brought about the humiliation of his plans for the 'Music of the future', as he called it, and forced his resignation from Weimar? It is a long and sordid story.

Inevitably Liszt's accomplishments at Weimar led to increasing hostility from the 'enemy' camps at Leipzig and Vienna. Hotbeds of conservatism, they watched with mounting concern as Liszt consolidated his revolution at Weimar. They would have no part of the 'new music' and fought it tooth and nail. To understand their attitude we have to go back to 1834 when Schumann founded a magazine called the *Neue Zeitschrift für Musik*. It was a progressive journal which supported the cause of the young romantics against the old reactionaries—the 'Band of David' against the 'Philistines' as Schumann put it. In 1844 Schumann resigned the editorship. The following year he was succeeded by Franz Brendel, an ardent Lisztian. The magazine now became a mouthpiece for the 'Neo-German' School and began to pour out a flood of propaganda on its behalf. Schumann, who had never been a supporter of Liszt, was appalled. The parties now divided and took up firmly entrenched positions. Brahms, after a brief flirtation with Weimar, broke with the Neo-Germans, and fell in behind Schumann. Anyway, he had disgraced himself at the Altenburg when Liszt had turned round in the middle of a performance of his B minor Sonata and seen Brahms asleep! But worse was to come. Wagner, one of Liszt's staunchest allies, published a spiteful article in the *Neue Zeitschrift* on 'The Jews in Music.' Unfortunately, Liszt's orchestral leader at Weimar was the great Jewish violinist Joachim, a close friend of both Schumann and Brahms. Mortally offended, he resigned his position at Weimar.

This, then, was roughly how things stood in 1853. Now followed a series of misfortunes which seriously affected Liszt's career, and which are indirectly attributable to these early differences with Brahms and Schumann. When his symphonic poem *Mazeppa* was performed at Leipzig, it was greeted with catcalls and boos. Even more humiliating was the failure of the 'Dante' Symphony when it was played at Dresden in 1857. The climax of the wretched business came in 1860 when Liszt read in the Berlin newspaper *Das Echo* a strongly-worded manifesto directed against the theories fostered at Weimar and signed by Brahms and Joachim among others. It was a foolish document and brought no credit to its signatories. Liszt chose to keep silent throughout the entire quarrel. It is significant, though, that he never played a single work of Brahms in public.

In Weimar itself, Liszt's position was continually undermined by the vicious gossip surrounding his association with the Princess. Her divorce looked as far distant as ever. The good citizens of Weimar began to wonder how long they would have to tolerate her as Liszt's mistress. She was not popular; Carolyne made no secret of her dislike of the strait-laced Germans. Moreover, she was an embarrassment to the Weimar Court which had succumbed to mounting pressure from Tsar Nicholas I to ban Carolyne from all court functions—a rebuff which reflected as much on Liszt as on the Princess. What made Liszt's standing with the Weimar Court all the more delicate was his friendship with Richard Wagner. In 1849, Wagner had taken part in the Dresden uprising. It was quickly put down by loyalist troops, but a warrant was issued for Wagner's arrest as the authorities regarded him as a dangerous revolutionary. Outlawed from every state in Germany he made his way secretly to Liszt who sheltered him in the Altenburg; with typical magnanimity, Liszt helped to organize Wagner's escape route to Switzerland and sent him on his way with a handsome loan. Thereafter, Liszt never failed to champion Wagner's artistic cause. He mounted the first performance of *Lohengrin* at Weimar in 1850 at a time when it could hardly have been politically expedient to do so. Later on came performances of Wagner's *Flying Dutchman*. The Weimar Court knew full well of Liszt's association with Wagner. Publicly, they turned a blind eye to it; privately, however, it must have caused them some misgivings. It put them in a false light. To their neighbouring states, they appeared to be promoting a man wanted for subversive activities. There is little doubt that during his Weimar years the Wagner connection continually jeopardized Liszt's position.

Insult was now added to injury. Liszt was subjected to harassment in carrying out his plans at Weimar by the Intendant Dingelstedt, a minor court official, recently appointed manager of the Weimar opera-house. He had no time for Liszt's grandiose schemes which cost the state a great deal of money. Had the Grand Duke and Duchess still been alive things might have been different; but they had both died in 1853, and their son and successor the Grand Duke Karl Alexander was so involved with matters of state that Dingelstedt found himself unexpectedly elevated to a position of some authority, and he began to meddle with Liszt's projected arrangements. He cut down on the number of music productions and put on a series of inferior plays.

By 1858, the situation was tense. At the first performance of Cornelius's opera *Barber of Baghdad*, which Liszt himself conducted, a demonstration was mounted against the work and Liszt was hissed. It was the last straw. Liszt handed in his resignation to the Grand Duke.

IV

Abbé Liszt

There is a story that Liszt once went to have his portrait painted by Ary Scheffer, a second-rate French artist. Liszt sat down and assumed his usual expression. Scheffer snapped at him angrily: 'Don't put on the airs of a man of genius with me; you know well enough that I'm not impressed by it.' To which Liszt quietly replied: 'You're perfectly right, my dear friend; but you must try to forgive me. You can't realize how it spoils one to have been an infant prodigy.'

'. . . to have been an infant prodigy'. As Liszt started to wind up his affairs at Weimar, he was in a mood of utter despair. He looked back over his twelve years at Weimar, years of intense activity, much of it in the service of others, and he could hardly believe that they had culminated in an expression of hostility against him. The contrast with his youthful triumphs, in the days when he could do no wrong, was almost too painful to contemplate. Thanks to Weimar, he had made powerful enemies. His plans for the 'music of the future' had crumbled to dust.

Liszt's gloom was further darkened by a personal sorrow. He received news of the death, in 1859, of his young son Daniel. The boy was only nineteen, and had been studying law in Vienna. Although Liszt had seen little of him in recent years, he was deeply attached to him and took the news badly.

Altogether, this was a time of spiritual crisis for Liszt, and he had to face it alone. The Princess had left Weimar and gone to Rome in a last effort to expedite her divorce. In her absence, Liszt made his Will. The document throws a flood of light on his troubled frame of mind.

This is my testament
I write it on the date of 14th September (1860), when the Church celebrates the elevation of the Holy Cross. The name of this feast also expresses the ardent and mysterious emotion which, like the sacred stigmata, has transpierced my entire life.

69

Yes, Christ crucified, the 'foolishness' and the elevation of the Cross, this was my true vocation. I have felt it to the depths of my heart from the age of seventeen, when with tears and supplications I begged to be permitted to enter the seminary in Paris, and I hoped that it would be given to me to live the life of the saints and perhaps die the death of the martyrs. It has not been so, alas! But never since, through the many sins and errors that I have committed and for which I am sincerely repentant and contrite, has the divine light of the Cross been wholly withdrawn from me. Sometimes it has even flooded my whole soul with its glory. I thank God for it, and I shall die with my soul attached to the Cross, our redemption, our supreme beatitude; and to render a testimony to my faith, I desire to receive the sacraments of the Catholic, Apostolic and Roman Church before my death, and thus obtain the remission and absolution of my sins. Amen.

He had obviously experienced a powerful resurgence of the religious fervour which had gripped him as a youth. We shall discover that this eventually led him into one of the most solemn turning-points of his life.

He goes on to write about his friendship for Wagner and pours out his heart over the petty intrigues that had brought his championship of that composer's music to an abrupt end.

There is in contemporary art one name that is already glorious and will be more and more so: Richard Wagner. His genius has been a torch to me; I have followed it, and my friendship for Wagner has retained all the character of a noble passion. At one time (some ten years ago), I dreamed of a new epoch for Weimar comparable to that of Karl August, an epoch which Wagner and I were to be the coryphaei, as Goethe and Schiller once were. The meanness, not to say the villainy, of certain local circumstances, all sorts of jealousies and absurdities elsewhere as well as here, have prevented the realization of this dream which would have redounded to the honour of the present Grand Duke.

Liszt spent the next few months nostalgically sorting through his papers, burning old letters, and packing his belongings. He loved the Altenburg, and now he had to leave it. He wrote to the Princess:

It is impossible for me to tell you all the emotions of my last hours at the Altenburg. Each room, each piece of furniture, down, even, to the steps of the staircase and to the green lawns of the garden, all was illuminated by your love, without which I feel annihilated. I could not keep back my tears.

On 20 October 1861 Liszt arrived in Rome. The Vatican, after long consideration of the case, was prepared to grant Carolyne an annulment of her first marriage, and her wedding to Liszt was fixed for 22 October, Liszt's fiftieth birthday. The little church of San Carlo al Corso was chosen for the ceremony and decked out with flowers for the occasion. At the last moment, however, there came a touch of high drama. An emissary arrived from the Vatican late on the eve of the wedding, to inform the Princess that there had been some second thoughts and that permission was now revoked. The Wittgenstein family, it seemed, were raising new objections which had to be studied. Carolyne was dumbfounded. For fifteen years she had fought incessantly for the right to marry Liszt. She had this right within her grasp, only to see it dashed to the ground by the secret intrigues of the higher clergy. We shall probably never know the full story. Incredibly, it later transpired that Carolyne's husband, Nicholas, had obtained a divorce from her in Russia as early as 1855, and had remarried without the Princess being informed of the fact. Rome must have known the true situation, but for reasons of expediency chose to keep silent about it. Carolyne had enemies in high places.

As for Liszt, he might well have been relieved that the wretched business was finally settled. Cornelius was forthright in expressing the view that Liszt's desire to marry the Princess was half-hearted. Cosima, his daughter, put it more strongly, saying that her father looked forward to the marriage 'as to a burial service'. Significantly, when Nicholas died in 1864, and the last obstacle to their union was removed, there was no further talk of marriage between them.

For the time being, Liszt decided to settle in Rome. He had always loved the city. Moreover, he was uncertain what the future held for him. He took rooms at 113 Via Felice. Every evening he visited Carolyne who had moved into a separate apartment. These visits were not ones he cherished. Since the wedding fiasco their relationship had changed. Carolyne had become an eccentric. Still smarting from the Vatican's *volte face* she was obsessed with Canon Law. Her rooms were filled with theological tomes over which she pored incessantly. She was preparing herself for the task of writing her magnum opus which rejoiced in the title of *The Interior Causes of the External Weaknesses of the Roman Catholic Church*. This monumental project was to take twenty-five years to write; Carolyne completed it only a fortnight before she died. It ran into twenty-four volumes and it is virtually unreadable. The book was really a therapy, so to speak, a gigantic rationalization of her differences with the theologians. She paced the floor incessantly while writing it, smoking her black cigars. No fresh air was allowed into the apartment and the atmosphere was choking. The curtains were always drawn, even against the daylight, and the gloomy interior was perpetually lit by flickering candles. No wonder Liszt began to see less of her. To the end of her days she remained a recluse.

Liszt now entered the blackest and most troubled phase of his life. He suffered a marked personality change. His sense of boundless optimism temporarily deserted him. He became introspective. His hair turned grey and on his face appeared the warts with which everybody who has seen photographs of Liszt in later life is familiar. He was vividly described by Gregorovius in his *Roman Journal* of April 1862 as 'tall, thin, with long grey hair . . . he is burnt out . . . only the outer walls remain, from whence a little ghostlike flame hisses forth'. Personal tragedy again left its mark. In September 1862 his eldest daughter Blandine died in childbirth aged twenty-six. She had been happily married to a Parisian lawyer, Emile Ollivier, who later became the French Prime Minister. Coming so soon after the death of Daniel, Blandine's death was a great blow to Liszt. Of his three children, only Cosima now survived and she was to become a perpetual cross to him.

It was in an attempt to bring some repose into his unsettled life that in 1863 Liszt entered the little monastery of Madonna del Rosario as a guest of the Dominican friars. The monastery, which was situated on a hill just outside Rome, and enjoyed wonderful views across the city, had an air of indescribable calm about it. In this peaceful retreat Liszt spent his time in meditation, preparing himself for one of the gravest decisions of his life. He had resolved to enter the lower orders of the priesthood.

How can we explain Liszt's longing to become a priest? On the face of it, it is a bizarre paradox. Here was a supreme man-of-the-world who had rubbed shoulders with kings and princes; most of his life he had commanded considerable luxury, not to say power; he had only to open a piano and audiences swooned; he had enjoyed the favours of beautiful women, setting all Europe by the ears with the scandal of it; there had been illegitimate children. How could such a man become a priest? Yet the more we know of Liszt, the more we realize that nothing could have been more in keeping with his character than the priesthood. Ever since childhood, a powerful mystical streak had been at work in Liszt's personality; his youthful encounter with the Abbé Lammenais had filled him with humanitarian ideals; he had given generously in time and wealth to any and every cause; he was a devout Catholic; the desire to renounce the world had always been strong within him. To rephrase the question: How could such a man *not* become a priest? Predictably, Liszt was accused of lack of sincerity. His detractors, doubtless recalling his clanking medals, his sword of honour and Lola Montez, took it to be a superb *coup de théâtre* by the master showman. The charge will hardly bear close scrutiny, however. Liszt had pondered his decision for years. When the moment came, he acted with the inner conviction of a man who has looked into his own soul and seen that no other alternative is possible to him. As he himself put it, his decision agreed with all the antecedents of his youth. He confessed in his Will that he had felt the Church to be his true vocation 'from the age of seventeen when, with tears and supplications I begged to be permitted to enter the seminary in Paris, and I hoped that it would be given to me to live the life of the saints and perhaps die the death of the martyrs'. This youthful longing had been firmly suppressed by Anna, his mother, but throughout the years it had never been entirely extinguished in him. Anna burst into tears when she heard of his decision. The child, after all, had become father to the man. Liszt wrote to her:

> You know, dearest mother, how during the years of my youth, I dreamed myself incessantly into the world of the saints. Nothing seemed to me so self-evident as heaven, nothing so true and so rich in blessedness as the goodness and compassion of God. Notwithstanding all the aberrations and errors of my life, nothing and nobody have ever been able to shake my faith in immortality and eternal salvation, a faith I had won by my prayers in the Churches at Raiding and Frauendorf, the Mariahilf Church in Vienna, Nôtre-Dame de Lorette and Saint-Vincent de Paule in Paris. . . . When I now read the lives of the saints I feel I am meeting again, after a long journey, old and revered friends from whom I shall never part.

Liszt entered the ecclesiastical state on 25 April 1865 in the chapel of H.S.H. Monseigneur Hohenlohe at the Vatican. He later wrote:

> Convinced as I was that this act would strengthen me in the right road, I accomplished it without effort, in all simplicity and uprightness of intention. Moreover, it agrees with the antecedents of my youth . . .
> To speak familiarly, if 'the cloak does not make the monk', it also does

not prevent him from being one; and, in certain cases, when the monk is already formed within, why not appropriate the outer garment of one?

But I am forgetting that I do not in the least intend to become a monk, in the severe sense of the word. For this I have no vocation.

The extent to which Liszt had committed himself to the Church must be clearly understood. There was nothing irrevocable about it. He took only four of the seven orders of priesthood. He could not celebrate Mass, nor could he hear confession. He undertook no vows of celibacy. At any time he was free to retract. His letter makes it perfectly clear that he had no intention of going further than this.

While Liszt was in the monastery of the Madonna del Rosario he was given his own cell, in which he was free to meditate and work, and he also had a piano. It became his habit to rise before dawn, attend mass, and then compose for several hours. On one occasion Pope Pius IX visited him in his cell, a rare honour, and requested that Liszt play to him. This he did with such beautiful effect that the Pontiff was moved to tears. The old magician had not lost his cunning. Among the compositions Liszt completed in the monastery are two remarkable pieces of music: the two Franciscan Legends. The first one bears the title *St. Francis of Assisi preaching to the birds*. Liszt had in mind the charming legend of Francis of Assisi who beheld the multitude of birds which filled the wayside and was moved to preach to them. 'And forthwith those which were in the trees came around him, and not one moved during the whole sermon; nor would they fly away until the Saint had given them his blessing.' It is an evocative story, and Liszt matched it with an equally evocative piece of bird-song in which we hear the chirping and twittering birds gradually give way to the 'sermon'. Liszt apologizes in his Preface for his 'lack of ingenuity' in capturing this remarkable scene. In fact, Liszt reveals such skill in conjuring up bird sounds that the work must be regarded as the historical link between Couperin's *Le Coucou* and Messiaen's *Catalogue d'Oiseaux*.

The other legend is called *St. Francis of Paola walking on the waters*. The story tells of St. Francis of Paola being turned away by the boatman at the ferry-crossing of the Straits of Messina because he could not afford the fare. 'If he is a saint,' remarked the boatman, 'let him walk.' Whereupon St. Francis stepped upon the waters and walked safely across the Straits to the other side. We hear the menacing sounds of the waves and the tremendous swell of the waters, and through it all there sounds the 'St. Francis' theme

74

floating serenely across the seascape. There was a picture of this scene hanging in Liszt's study at Weimar. St. Francis of Paola, incidentally, was Liszt's patron saint, which may have been one reason why he retained a special affection for this piece until the end of his days.

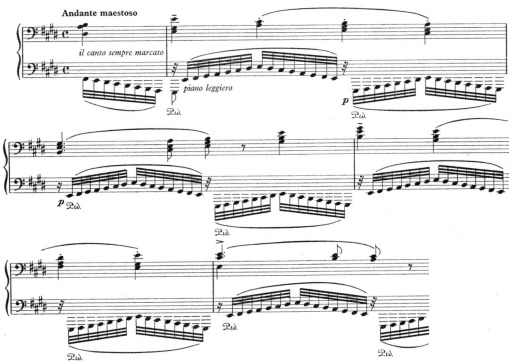

Legend: St. Francis of Paola walking on the waters

In 1865, while Liszt was still at Rome, he completed his remarkable series of transcriptions of the Beethoven symphonies. The task had occupied him, on and off, for many years. Nobody understood the art of the piano transcription better than Liszt, yet even he regarded these symphonies as an almost insuperable challenge to one pair of hands. In his Preface to the collection, Liszt declared his aim.

I confess that I should have to regard it a rather useless employment of my time, if I had but added one more to the numerous hitherto published piano arrangements, following in their rut; but I consider my time well employed if I have succeeded in transferring to the piano not only the grand outlines of Beethoven's compositions but also those numerous fine details, and smaller traits that so powerfully contribute to the completion of the ensemble.

Liszt was not content, then, merely to reduce Beethoven's symphonies to two staves, after the manner of the 'hack' arranger. What he wanted was a genuine 'translation' from one medium to the other, a 'translation' which would not only adhere faithfully to Beethoven's original but which would remain eminently playable. The results are almost miraculous, and these transcriptions have remained an impeccable model of their kind down to the present day. Sir Donald Tovey said of them that 'they prove conclusively .... that Liszt was by far the most wonderful interpreter of orchestral scores on the pianoforte the world is ever likely to see'.

Consider Liszt's transcription of the *Eroica* Symphony. Time and again, Liszt sees straight into the heart of an 'impossible' passage, and he succeeds in solving the problem of how to transcribe it for the piano so admirably that he reproduces the Symphony's complex textures on the keyboard without harming Beethoven's thought in the slightest degree. One has only to compare Liszt's transcription with a standard piano arrangement of the same work. Take the great climax of the *Eroica's* 'Marche Funèbre', for instance. This is how Liszt tackles the passage:

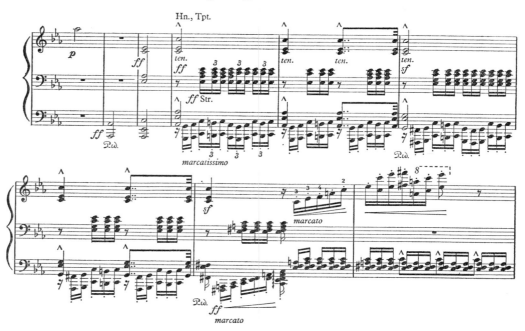

It looks formidable, set out on three staves. Yet on analysis it turns out to be eminently playable. Furthermore, it has all the power and force of Beethoven's original texture. These are the very qualities the following routine arrangement lacks.

Both versions, of course, should be compared with the full score of Beethoven's original. Only then can Liszt's achievement be fully appreciated.

These transcriptions show Liszt in an unfamiliar light. They completely dispel the popular view of Liszt as a showman, taking other composers' works and turning them into a fireworks display for his own glorification. In fact, the act of self-denial Liszt here discloses, suppressing his own immense creative impulses in the interests of Beethoven's music, is almost without parallel.

Liszt's violent quarrel with Wagner dates from his Roman period. It was so serious that the two men had nothing to do with one another for six years. At the centre of it all was Liszt's daughter Cosima.

Cosima was nineteen when, in 1857, she married Liszt's favourite pupil, Hans von Bülow. The young couple had met in Berlin a year or two earlier when Cosima had started taking piano lessons from Hans. They quickly fell in love. When Liszt heard about it he was delighted and readily agreed to the wedding; he himself attended the ceremony. Within a short time there were two children by the marriage. To all outward appearances it was a perfect match. But Cosima became unsettled. She had a great deal of her father's restless temperament. She also had a will of iron. Soon, she was harbouring a secret desire—for Liszt's friend Richard Wagner. This was to have untold consequences for all parties concerned, including Liszt himself.

Wagner's own first marriage had ended, after a series of bitter quarrels, in a permanent separation from his wife Minna in 1861. He had met Cosima through Liszt, of course, and he can hardly have been blind to the extent of the young woman's infatuation for him. In 1863, Wagner visited Berlin. While Bülow was rehearsing, Wagner and Cosima went for a drive together. Infatuation blossomed into love. The following year Wagner went to Munich, the guest of Ludwig II of Bavaria who was obsessed with Wagner's music. Ludwig had placed unlimited resources at Wagner's disposal and was intent on keeping him at his court. It was a simple matter for Wagner to persuade Ludwig to offer Bülow an attractive post in Munich. No student of Wagner would assume that he did this out of charity. With the Bülows duly installed in Munich, Wagner had ready access to Cosima. By 1865 they were lovers and Cosima gave birth to Wagner's child. Bülow was completely humiliated. After several attempts to patch things up, he suffered a nervous breakdown and eventually abandoned Cosima to her lover. He divorced her in 1870.

Liszt was disturbed at this turn of events. He was fond of Bülow and disliked seeing him hurt. In 1867, Cosima gave birth to another child, Eva, and Liszt was galvanized into action. He travelled to the Villa Triebschen, near Lucerne, where Cosima and Wagner now lived, to thrash things out with them. The interview was a stormy one. Afterwards, all Liszt would say about it was that it was as if he had seen Napoleon on St. Helena. It appears that Cosima was more than a match for her father, and even outclassed Wagner in her range of invective. She threw Liszt's own chequered career in his face. Was she not his own illegitimate offspring? Who was he to lay down the law? The argument was unanswerable. Six years passed before Liszt had anything further to do with his wayward daughter and Richard Wagner.

The reason for Liszt's agitation is obvious. In 1863, as we have seen, he had entered the monastery of the Madonna del Rosario as a novice. That was the very year Cosima and Wagner had declared their love. As the gossip gathered about his daughter, Liszt was mortified. He could hardly avoid mixing in musical circles where the latest scandal was freely discussed. He was finding it difficult enough to live down his own past life without having to live down Cosima's as well. Just as Liszt was trying to impress on his clerical advisors his suitability for admission into holy orders, tongues were wagging all over Rome about Cosima's to-ings and fro-ings with Wagner. At any rate, Liszt could reflect ironically, it made a change from Carolyne. The finishing touch came, as we saw, in 1865, when Liszt received the tonsure of the Roman Catholic Church, and Cosima, with a nice sense of timing, presented her father with an illegitimate grand-daughter.

All these events—his thwarted marriage to Carolyne, the death of two of his children, his break with Wagner and Cosima, and the apparent failure of his Weimar achievement—hung like a shadow over his life. They left an indelible stamp on his personality. He became old in Rome, borne down by the sheer weight of it all. It was not being permitted to him to enter his final years peacefully. The accounts we have of Liszt at this time testify to his gaunt appearance, his craggy features and his, by now, white hair. In Rome, he became a familiar sight; he cut a striking figure as he strode through the streets in his black cassock, with his white hair streaming in the wind. Gregorovius once spotted him getting out of a hackney carriage and described him unforgettably as 'Mephistopheles disguised as an Abbé'.

During his Roman period Liszt struck up one of the closest friendships of his old age with Monseigneur Hohenlohe who, it will be remembered, had officiated at the ceremony at which Liszt was received into the Church. There was already a close bond between the two men; Hohenlohe's brother, Prince Constantine, had married Carolyne's daughter, Marie, who was brought up in Liszt's household at Weimar, and whom Liszt had almost come to regard as his own child. A man of considerable personal wealth, Hohenlohe had recently been made a cardinal and he now offered to place at Liszt's disposal a suite of rooms in his magnificent home at Tivoli, the Villa d'Este. Even today, the Villa d'Este still has some of the most beautiful gardens in the world; its huge cypresses are among the wonders of nature, while its hundreds of splashing fountains form a spectacle unmatched anywhere. Here, at the Villa d'Este, Liszt spent some of the happiest moments of his old age. He used to call the Villa his 'El Dorado'. He would sometimes sit in the gardens for hours, lost in contemplation, and some of the finest compositions of his last few years were conceived there. From about 1867 Liszt spent several months of each year, from July to November, living and working at the Villa d'Este which became a kind of spiritual home to him.

In 1867, Liszt unexpectedly received an invitation to visit Budapest. The

Abbé Liszt

Austrian Emperor Franz-Josef was about to be crowned King of Hungary and Liszt, as Hungary's leading composer, was asked to write a work for the celebrations. He gladly accepted the invitation; within the remarkably short space of three weeks he had composed his *Hungarian Coronation Mass* and hurried off to Budapest to conduct it. He had not been to his native land for years, not since his hey-day as a performer in fact, and the Hungarians gave this living legend one of the most remarkable receptions of his entire career. It seems that after the coronation ceremony thousands of people had lined the main road leading from the church of St. Matthias in the expectation of seeing the new king walk in procession. There was some delay, and just as the suspense was becoming unbearable, Liszt accidentally appeared walking down the road which had been specially cordoned off for royalty, resplendent in his soutane which was covered in decorations. He was recognized at once, and a great murmur of approval swept through the crowds. As he walked down the road, tens of thousands of people took up the applause which swelled to a tumult. No playwright could have staged the scene more effectively. For many people in that vast throng Liszt, the greatest living Hungarian, *was* the king, while the foreigner Franz-Josef who belatedly brought up the rear, symbolized nothing but the despised Austrian tyranny of which all Hungarians longed to rid themselves.

After this visit to Budapest Liszt became increasingly involved in the artistic life of his native country. Hungary had suddenly reminded him that he was, after all, Hungarian: he returned there frequently in the years to

'Long live Franz Liszt':
a drawing given to Liszt on his birthday

come. From this time, too, dates his renewed interest in Hungarian national music which was to lead to some of the most astonishing and unexpected creations of his old age.

Liszt's dedication of his Sonata in B minor to Schumann

V

The Final Years

Ever since Liszt had left Weimar, the Grand Duke had been tactfully trying to arrange for his return. Liszt was missed there. At long last people were beginning to realize that he had brought honour and prestige to the town. True, there had been bitterness on both sides; but that was nearly ten years ago. The old antagonisms were dying down. There was now a growing fund of goodwill towards the man who had put Weimar on the map, musically speaking, and a move was made to see whether Liszt could be persuaded to return.

Liszt's reaction was predictable, and in keeping with everything we know of the man's generous nature. He was content to let bygones be bygones. But what kind of an association? The Grand Duke's suggestion was a simple one. Liszt should start masterclasses in piano-playing. In the old days, his pupils at the Altenburg had included such giants as Tausig and Bülow. But since then, a new and formidable generation of pianists had appeared. Most of them had never heard Liszt play a note, let alone received a lesson from him. But they revered his name, which had become part of the mythology of the piano, so to speak. As soon as it was announced that Liszt was about to return to Weimar to teach, young pianists the world over packed their bags and started to converge on Weimar in readiness for the master's arrival.

There was no question of Liszt's taking up residence at the Altenburg again. For one thing, the house would have been far too big for his modest needs; gone were the days when he liked to surround himself with ostentation. For another, the Grand Duke wished to do nothing that would remind people of Liszt's unpopular association with the Princess. So it was finally decided to place the Hofgärtnerei—the Court Gardener's house—at Liszt's disposal. This was ideal for his purpose. The Hofgärtnerei was a small, two-storey villa, surrounded on three sides by gardens, and therefore well secluded. The Grand Duchess herself supervised the decorations and furnishing, everything being set out to Liszt's own taste. A large music-room dominated the first floor with tall windows overlooking the gardens. In the middle of the room stood a grand piano. This room was to be the scene of the most famous piano classes in history. For seventeen years Liszt was to teach there. A stream of brilliant pupils passed through his hands, including Rosenthal, Sauer, Siloti, d'Albert and Lamond, in fact every pianist of note who appeared before the public between 1870 and 1900.

Although Liszt had taught since he was a youth living in Paris, by no stretch of the imagination could he be described as a pedagogue. He had no 'method', no 'system', no technical advice of any kind to offer his pupils. Not for him an analytical pursuit into the processes of piano-playing. Frankly, the subject bored him. 'Do I care how quickly you can play octaves?' he once shouted at a pupil renowned for his dexterity. The last thing the supreme master of the piano was concerned with when he himself played was the physical problems associated with the instrument. Consequently, as they no longer existed for him, he had long since ceased to consider them. Technical drudgery was a matter for each individual to cope with in his own way and in his own time. As Liszt himself put it, he expected his pupils to 'wash their dirty linen at home'. Of course, by observing Liszt himself play—watching the lie of his hands on the keyboard, seeing how certain passages were fingered, studying his pedal-effects—his pupils undoubtedly received the best possible guidance, and they learned far more than they might have done from a dry, academic description of these events.

All this was in marked contrast to Liszt's contemporaries, some of whom were obsessed with technical gimmickry. Kalkbrenner, for instance, had invented a 'hand-rail' for the express purpose of making the wrists and arms conform to the 'correct' lateral playing motions; it was an evil invention which wrecked many a promising career before it had properly begun. Kullak frowned on surplus movement of any kind and encouraged his pupils to practise with a coin balanced on the back of the hand. It was difficult to know what this dubious trick was meant to achieve except, as somebody wrily observed, to give people plenty of practice in bending down to pick up fallen coins off the floor. These things, 'mechanical aids', seemed to be fashionable. Even Schumann, in his younger days, had devised a sling for strengthening the fourth finger of his right hand, and had permanently damaged the tendons, forcing him to abandon all thoughts of becoming a performer.

What made Liszt's classes so exceptional was their emphasis on music. Liszt was concerned with interpretation, with performance. He would take apart a Beethoven sonata phrase by phrase, in an effort to get his pupils to comprehend the meaning behind the notes. In doing so, he established traditions of performance which survive to the present time. The classes were quite informal and held in a relaxed atmosphere. They usually took place in the afternoons, and sometimes as many as a dozen students would be present. The custom was for one pupil to play, Liszt and the others looking on, after which Liszt would make observations about the performance and perhaps even play through the work himself. These were moments to treasure, and the atmosphere could become electric on those occasions when Liszt, displeased with the way a performance was going, would push the pupil off the stool in an attempt to revive the flagging music. The whole keyboard would sometimes thunder and lighten, and the trembling student would get a glimpse into a mighty conception of the work which, until then, lay locked up behind the notes of the music. Liszt was an inspirational force. Simply to be in the same room with him, as more than one pupil testified, turned one, temporarily, into a better pianist.

The best account of Liszt at the Hofgärtnerei comes from an American pupil, Amy Fay, who travelled from the States in 1869 to study in Germany and first encountered Liszt in 1873.

> Yesterday I had prepared for him his *Au Bord d'une Source*. I was nervous and played badly. He was not to be put out, however, but acted as if he thought I had played charmingly, and then he sat down and played the piece himself, oh, *so* exquisitely! It made me feel like a wood-chopper. The notes just seemed to ripple off his fingers' ends with scarce any perceptible motion. As he neared the close I remarked that that funny little expression came over his face which he always has when he means to surprise you, and he suddenly took an unexpected chord and extemporised a poetical little end, quite different from the written one. Do you wonder people go distracted over him?

Amy Fay also gives a lively pen-portrait of Liszt:

> Liszt is the most interesting and striking looking man imaginable. Tall and slight, with deep-set eyes, shaggy eyebrows, and long iron-gray hair, which he wears parted in the middle. His mouth turns up at the corners, which gives him a most crafty and Mephistophelian expression when he smiles, and his whole appearance and manner have a sort of Jesuitical elegance and ease. His hands are very narrow, with long and slender fingers that look as if they had twice as many joints as other people's.

They are so flexible and supple that it makes you nervous to look at them. Anything like the polish of his manner I never saw.

During the two months of the year that Liszt was in residence at Weimar, the town inevitably filled up with students, for it was Liszt's rule never to turn anyone away. From dozens of lodgings there issued the constant noise of practising which posed such a serious nuisance to the residents that a by-law was actually passed by the town council, restricting piano practice to certain times of day, and then only with the windows shut! Liszt himself could often be seen walking down the street, with a group of pupils at his heels, talking as they went. There is a charming anecdote told by Strelezki, who was a pupil of Liszt from 1869 onwards. Strelezki was walking down the street when he collided with Liszt who was coming out of a cigar-shop. 'Lazybones!' exclaimed Liszt. 'You ought to be at home practising.' Strelezki explained that he had already done four hours' practice that morning, and was now on his way home to do more. 'In that case,' said Liszt, 'if you have already done four hours' slavery, come home with me.' Karl Heymann, another pupil, was with them, and as soon as they reached the Hofgärtnerei Liszt went straight to the piano and started playing. 'Karl,' he called out, 'what is that? It's been running through my head all afternoon, and I can't for the life of me think what it is.' Several times Liszt played the passage and eventually Strelezki thought he recognized it and suggested that it came from Balakirev's *Islamey*. 'Bravo! Bravo!' shouted Liszt. 'Of course it does. I haven't heard it since Tausig studied it with me and it has haunted me all afternoon.' The story indicates the degree of informality and friendliness that existed between Liszt and his pupils, quite unusual for those times. Altogether, the atmosphere at Weimar was delightful, and those who were fortunate enough to study with Liszt at this time carried away with them a rich store of experience which would remain with them for a lifetime.

Inevitably, there were those who took advantage of Liszt's generosity, and among his so-called pupils were a number of 'hangers-on' who were totally devoid of talent. Liszt tolerated them, but in at least one case it was to cost him dear. Although Liszt was now in his late fifties, and a man of the Church, he had lost none of his fatal attraction for women. More than one young female pupil lost her head over him. With one exception, however, there were to be no serious affairs. The exception, and that was a notable one, was Olga Janina, the self-styled 'Cossack Countess'. Olga was one of the most colourful of all the characters to present themselves to Liszt as a prospective 'pupil'. Practically all the information we have about her comes from her two autobiographical novels, *Souvenirs d'une Cosaque* and *Souvenirs d'une pianiste*, which she wrote under the pseudonym 'Robert Franz'. Olga Janina was born in the Ukraine. She first encountered Liszt in Rome in 1869 when she was about nineteen years old. Young in years, she already had a chequered career behind her. She had married at fifteen, but on the morning after her marriage she had horse-whipped her husband and left him. She fancied herself as a pianist, and after a brief spell at the Kiev Conservatoire she heard about Liszt and travelled all the way to Rome to meet him. She quickly developed a 'crush' on him, and Liszt had the greatest difficulty in shaking her off. Excitable and nervous, she was the type who created 'scenes', and Liszt kept up the relationship as much to spare himself possible embarrassment as to spare her feelings. At one point he managed to escape to the Villa d'Este; but Olga pursued him there and entered the grounds disguised as a gardenboy. There was a confrontation and, if her own account of the story is to be believed, Liszt surrendered to her. Obviously, the relationship could not be allowed to continue, particularly with the Princess Wittgenstein living almost within earshot. Liszt left for Budapest, but the 'Countess' came after him and burst into his apartment brandishing a revolver, threatening to shoot Liszt and then take poison. Liszt succeeded in calming her down and wrested the revolver from her. After this episode, she seems to have left his life as abruptly as she entered it. Eventually, she changed her name to 'Robert Franz' and revenged herself on Liszt by

Reminiscences

writing the above-mentioned novels, in which the revolver story and many other colourful tales are recounted in full.

Meanwhile, his Weimar activities notwithstanding, the Hungarians were intent on getting Liszt to spend more time in Budapest. The Government had set aside funds for the foundation of a new Academy of Music and Liszt was approached for his help and advice in getting the institution on its feet. It was a project which was close to his heart, for Hungary at that time had nowhere for the training of its young musicians, and Liszt resolved to devote some time and energy to the task. From 1872, until he died, Liszt spent the first three months of each year in Budapest. The 'Franz Liszt Academy of Music' was finally opened in 1875, thanks largely to his inexhaustible energy, and it still flourishes to this day as one of the leading musical establishments of the western world.

Liszt's life was now taking on a definite pattern. Each year was divided equally between Weimar, Rome and Budapest. From January to March he lived in Budapest; between April and June he taught at Weimar; then, from July to November, he stayed at the Villa d'Este near Rome. The distances were enormous. In those days it took sixty hours to travel from Rome to Budapest, and it was almost as long again to get from Budapest to Weimar. Yet this was to be the endless circle of his life—Budapest, Weimar, Rome— until the end of his days. Liszt called it *une vie trifurquée*—'a life split in three'.

Nothing is more remarkable in the whole of Liszt's creative output than the series of pieces he composed during the last ten years of his life. If he had written nothing else, he would still be an extraordinary composer. The picture Liszt's contemporaries had of him during this period was that of an eccentric old man, whiling away his time at the keyboard, composing 'difficult' music that few people could understand and fewer still wanted to hear. Critics like Hanslick and Esser poured such a flood of invective on these late works that it would have wrung a reply from a lesser man. But Liszt's 'answer' was to go on composing music ever more modern in outlook. The question arises: who was Liszt addressing in these final years? In a letter to the Princess Wittgenstein Liszt wrote that his one remaining ambition was 'to throw a lance as far as possible into the boundless realm of the future'. On another occasion, the seventy-four-year-old Liszt turned to a pupil, August Stradal, and remarked: 'The time will yet come when my works are appreciated. True, it will be late for me because I shall no longer be with you.' The conclusion is inescapable. Liszt was deliberately setting himself to address the generations as yet unborn. That he succeeded is no longer a matter for debate. Both Bartók and Busoni, after studying the late works, came to the conclusion that Liszt was the true father of modern music.

During the years 1870 to 1880 Liszt brought to completion the third and final volume of his great collection of pieces called *Years of Pilgrimage*. These pieces represent a remarkable stylistic departure from the ones in the earlier volumes. They have an unmistakably modern ring about them; one or two of them still sound, more than eighty years later, as stark and uncompromising as when they were first written. Always in the vanguard of modern music, Liszt here gives us more than one prophetic glimpse into the future. Several of the pieces in this final volume were composed at the Villa d'Este, directly inspired by the famous gardens there. The best-known work in the collection is *The Fountains of the Villa d'Este*. Liszt used to sit for hours gazing at these fountains, spellbound by the play of their cascading waters. The result was a piece of musical impressionism so advanced for its time that for thirty years it had no successor until Ravel composed his *Jeux d'eau*, a work which would be unthinkable without Liszt's example. But whereas Ravel, the master impressionist, merely composed an ingenious piece of 'water music', Liszt succeeded in transcending simple visual imagery of this kind and turned his streaming fountains into mystical symbols, associating them with the well-known verse from the Gospel According to St. John, which he quotes in the score. 'But whosoever drinketh the water that I shall give him, shall never thirst; but the water that I shall give him shall be in him a well of water springing up into everlasting life.' The following passage gives one some idea of how close the aged Liszt was in spirit to the French Impressionists.

The Fountains of the Villa d'Este

As Busoni put it, the work has remained the model for all musical fountains which have flowed since then.

Another of the Villa d'Este pieces which Liszt included in the final volume of *Years of Pilgrimage* is called *By the Cypresses of the Villa d'Este* (Threnody II). It is said that Liszt spent many hours during the warm Italian nights sitting out of doors and contemplating these swaying trees by moonlight. They obsessed his thoughts and inspired him to compose some of the best music of his old age. More than one commentator has pointed out the likeness between the opening of this piece and Wagner's *Tristan*.

By the Cypresses of the Villa d'Este

It shows that Liszt occasionally looked back to Wagner as well as forward to him.

Two pieces which are typical products of Liszt's old age are the *Csárdás Macabre* and the *Bagatelle without Tonality*. Neither was published in Liszt's lifetime. The *Bagatelle*, in fact, had to wait until 1956 before it finally appeared, but that seems to be in keeping with what has been described as a 'conspiracy of silence' surrounding Liszt's late works.

Csárdás Macabre begins with this arresting passage in parallel fifths.

When the seventy-year-old wizard defiantly threw out this passage Debussy was still only nineteen years of age, a fact which brings home its originality. It is said that Liszt wrote the piece in order to spite the conservative Hanslick; but it seems unlikely that Hanslick ever heard it. The title *Csárdás Macabre*, incidentally, is explained by the second subject which is based on a deliberate distortion of the plainchant theme for the dead, the *Dies Irae*.

Bagatelle without Tonality

The Final Years

The *Bagatelle without Tonality* was composed in 1885, a few months before Liszt died. For many years the manuscript was lost. The title is Liszt's own. It reflects his lifelong interest in the problem of tonality and represents one of the very first attempts to 'stretch' tonality to a point where no definite key could be heard. When we listen to this forward-looking piece it is a salutary reminder of Liszt's historical importance, for it was written more than twenty years before Schoenberg composed the first official atonal work—his Second String Quartet (1906).

Perhaps it was due to the blank incredulity with which some of his later music met that Liszt eventually came to the conclusion that he would never be recognized as a major composer during his own lifetime. His correspondence on the subject makes this quite plain. In a letter to Jessie Laussot, a pupil, he summed up his plight.

> It seems to me that Mr. Litz [*sic*] is, as it were, always welcome when he appears at the piano (especially since he has made a profession of the contrary) but it is not permitted him to have anything to do with thinking and writing according to his own fancy.
>
> The result is that for some 15 years, so-called friends, as well as in-different and ill-disposed people on all sides, sing, enough to split your head, to this unhappy Mr. Litz [*sic*], who has nothing to do with it: 'Be a pianist, and nothing but that. How is it possible for you *not* to be a pianist?'

'How is it possible for you *not* to be a pianist?' The question recurred like a persistent leit-motif to haunt his old age. But Liszt was realistic enough to come to terms with it. As early as 1859, he was ironically referring to himself as 'that notorious non-composer Franz Liszt' in the Preface to the collected edition of the songs, which showed that he was well aware of how his critics regarded him even then; and the remark reveals a kind of wry humour which characterized all his later comments about his own work. The degree of negative criticism which Liszt endured during the last twenty years of his life, however, left a deeper mark than this. So sensitive did he become that he actually went out of his way to discourage performances of his own works, an unexpected aspect of his personality. He wrote to von Herbeck:

> With regard to performances of my work generally, my disposition and inclination are more than ever completely in the negative. It seems to me, now, high time that I should be forgotten.

91

Again, he could write to Jessie Laussot in the same vein:

> Knowing by experience with how little favour my works meet, I have been obliged to force a sort of systematic heedlessness on myself with regard to them, and a resigned passiveness. Thus, during my years of foreign activity in Germany, I constantly observed the rule of never asking anyone whatsoever to have any of my works performed; more than that, I plainly dissuaded many persons from doing so who showed some intention of this kind—and I shall do the same elsewhere.

The degree of self-effacement in these letters is quite considerable. It stands in marked contrast to the flamboyance of his youth. Anyone who studies the correspondence of Liszt's old age is bound to see him in a new light, and one which differs considerably from the conventional picture of him presented in the history books.

In 1872 Liszt patched up his historic quarrel with Wagner. It was Wagner who made the first move. Two years earlier he had married Cosima. Neither of them had thought fit to inform Liszt; the first he knew of it was when he read about the event in the newspapers. Wagner saw an opportunity to set wrongs to right on the occasion of the laying of the foundation-stone at Bayreuth. He badly wanted his old friend to be present at the ceremony which represented the crowning achievement of his life's work. Cosima, who had washed her hands of her father, was against the idea. But Wagner's desire to see Liszt once more proved irresistible. He wrote Liszt a letter which, while it must have broken his pride to write it, surely ranks among the most human and moving documents one composer ever addressed to another.

> My Great and Dear Friend,
>
> Cosima maintains that you would not come even if I were to invite you. We should have to endure that, as we have had to endure so many things! But I cannot forbear to invite you. And what is it I cry to you when I say 'Come'? You came into my life as the greatest man whom I could ever address as an intimate friend; you gradually went apart from me, perhaps because I had become less close to you than you were to me. In place of you there came to me your deepest new-born being and completed my longing to know you were very close to me. So you live in full beauty before me and in me, and we are one beyond the grave itself. You were the first to ennoble me by his love; to a second, higher life am I now wedded in *her*, and can accomplish what I should never have been

able to accomplish alone. Thus you could become everything to me, while I could remain so little to you: how immeasurably greater is my gain!

If now I say to you 'Come', I thereby say to you 'Come to yourself!' For it is yourself that you will find. Blessings and love to you, whatever decision you may come to!

Your old friend,

RICHARD

Liszt was too generous-hearted not to respond to Wagner on the same level. His reply of 20 May 1872 runs:

My Dear and Noble Friend,

I am too deeply moved by your letter to be able to thank you in words. But from the depths of my heart I hope that every shadow of a circumstance that could hold me fettered may disappear, and that soon we may see each other again. Then shall you see in perfect clearness how inseparable is my soul from *you both*, and how intimately I live again in that 'second' and higher life of yours in which you are able to accomplish what you could never have accomplished alone. Herein is Heaven's pardon for me: God's blessing on you both, and all my love.

These are extraordinarily moving letters. They deserve the closest study. For five years the two men had not seen each other, let alone corresponded. Yet the old fire of their friendship proved impossible to quench, and it burned as brightly as ever at the moment of Wagner's greatest triumph.

After this, Liszt became a frequent guest at the Villa Wahnfried at Bayreuth where Wagner now lived. The two composers spent many a contented hour together discussing music, with Liszt sometimes rounding off the evening after dinner with a performance of a Wagner score at the piano for the enjoyment of the assembled guests.

Two months before Wagner's death, Liszt actually had a premonition of it. The story comes from Liszt himself; it is an indication of how close the two composers had become. It was December 1882. Liszt was in Venice. The Wagners had invited him to spend the winter there with them. The funeral processions by gondola along the canals, which are a feature of the city to this day, came to fascinate him. The thought that Wagner himself might soon die, and his corpse float down the lagoons in this manner, began to exercise his imagination to a point where he had a revelation of Wagner's death. Under its impact he composed two extraordinary pieces: *La lugubre Gondola I and II.* Two months later, in fact, Wagner was dead, and his funeral procession glided down those same Venice canals just as Liszt imagined it would. News of his death was brought to Liszt in Budapest, to where he had meanwhile travelled. He is said to have been composing at his desk at the time, and he did not even look up and register surprise. But he was overheard to whisper brokenly to himself: 'He today, I tomorrow.'

Liszt's final years were not happy ones. Most of his closest friends were now dead, and he missed them. His health, until now perfect, was showing signs of strain. In 1881 he had taken a severe fall down the stairs of the Hofgärtnerei, and it took him some time to recover; he limped rather badly for several weeks afterwards. His vision was also deteriorating, a cataract having developed in one eye, and he was easily fatigued. He was also concerned about money problems. Since 1847 he had not earned a penny from piano playing, and as he always refused to accept a fee from his pupils he had virtually no income. During his Weimar period in the 1850s his salary amounted to no more than a meagre £200 ($550) a year. He had been financially responsible for his three children and had supported his ageing mother in Paris, all of which had helped to deplete his resources. As he gave money away freely to any cause, no matter how unworthy, his capital also dwindled. His only source of income was from his published compositions, but this gradually dried up as they became less popular and sold fewer copies. It was a ridiculous position to be in. Here was the world's greatest pianist. All he had to do was to announce a public concert and the money would come pouring in. But he always steadfastly refused to contemplate such an act. An amusing sidelight to his persistent refusal to return to the concert platform came in 1874 when the secretary of a musical festival about to be held in Liverpool wrote to Liszt to find out what was his fee! Liszt treated him gently but firmly.

Dear Sir,

Your kind communication rests upon a harmless mistake. You are presumably not aware that for twenty-six years I have altogether ceased to be regarded as a pianist, hence I have not for a long time given any concerts, and only very occasionally played the piano in public, for some very special reason, to aid some charity or to further some artistic object, and then only in Rome, in Hungary (my native country), and in Vienna —nowhere else. And on these rare and very exceptional occasions no one has ever dreamed of offering me any remuneration in money. Excuse me, therefore, dear sir, that I cannot accept your invitation to the Liverpool Musical Festival, inasmuch as I could not think of wearying the public with my piano playing.

As the year 1886 approached, the seventy-fifth anniversary of Liszt's birth, concerts began to be arranged in various parts of the world to celebrate the event. It became clear to Liszt that he could not possibly accept all the invitations which showered on him, some of which came from as far away as St. Petersburg. But one invitation he did accept. That was to London, where a performance of his Oratorio, *St. Elisabeth*, was to be presented in April at St. James's Hall, with Sir Alexander Mackenzie conducting. Liszt had not been to London for more than forty years, and the news of his impending visit was widely advertised there. On Saturday 3 April, Liszt landed at Dover where he was met by one of his English pupils, Walter Bache, who travelled to London on the train with him. The next few days were spent in a round of social activities. He visited the Royal Academy of Music on Wednesday 7 April for a concert of music after which Walter Bache formally presented the Liszt Scholarship and Liszt was persuaded to play. That same evening came the performance of *St. Elisabeth* after which Liszt received a standing ovation. On the Thursday a great reception was given in his honour at the Grosvenor Gallery. It was a glittering occasion and Liszt brought it to a rousing conclusion with a performance of his

Second Hungarian Rhapsody. The English critic, Fuller-Maitland, heard him play and wrote:

> His playing was a thing never to be forgotten or approached by later artists. The peculiar quiet brilliance of his rapid passages, the noble proportion kept between the parts and the meaning and effect which he put into the music were the most striking points.

During the next few days Liszt attended a concert at Crystal Palace, heard a Palestrina Mass at Brompton Oratory and went to the London début of his Scottish pupil, Frederic Lamond, at St. James's Hall. He also struck up an acquaintance with the great actor Henry Irving and attended a gala performance of *Faust* at the Lyceum Theatre. Altogether, his London visit was a memorable one—for London, as well as for Liszt—and he promised that he would return the following year, a promise which was not, alas, to be fulfilled. He left England at the end of April and journeyed first to Antwerp. He then went on to Paris, arriving there on 5 May for a further performance of *St. Elisabeth* and his *Gran Mass* which was given in the church of St. Eustache. By the middle of May he was back again in Weimar, after almost two months travelling, and had a well-earned rest in the Hofgärtnerei. He wrote to his pupil Sophie Menter about the various physical disabilities which had now overtaken him, and he mentioned an impending operation on his eyes by Gräfe, a Hallé surgeon. It was obvious that his health was deteriorating, but no one could have guessed just how near his end was. Despite not feeling well, he undertook a short excursion to Luxembourg in June, after which he planned to go by train to Bayreuth for the Wagner festival in July.

If the circumstantial account of Liszt's death, given by Julius Kapp, is true, it is a standing indictment against those who were in a position to ease his last moments.

Liszt arrived in Bayreuth for the Wagner celebrations on 21 July 1886. The long train journey upset him and he immediately took to his bed with a high fever and a racking cough. He had not been asked to stay at the Villa Wahnfried with Cosima and his grandchildren, so he took a room at 1 Siegfriedstrasse which was close by. For the first two days he was forced to stay indoors and scarcely anybody knew that he had arrived. On 23 July, although no better, he made a valiant effort to get up, and succeeded in attending the first of the *Parsifal* performances. Thoroughly exhausted, he spent part of the next day, Saturday, resting at Wahnfried. On the

Sunday there was a performance of *Tristan* and Liszt went to it because he had promised Cosima that he would. He sat at the back of the Wagner's family box, slumped in the shadows, with a handkerchief clasped to his mouth. Somebody spotted him when the lights went up during an interval, and he came forward to receive an ovation. It was the last time he was seen in public. He returned to his lodgings and took to his sick-bed, never to get up again. Cosima had her hands full with the administration of the festival and was slow to grasp the seriousness of the situation. Every morning she called in to bring Liszt his coffee and then left. Unfortunately, the food provided at his lodgings was unsuitable and he was left alone all day with nothing to eat as everybody was at the theatre. On Monday, the 26th, the doctor was called in and committed the elementary blunder of prohibiting alcohol. For years, Liszt had consumed brandy as a matter of routine, and the abrupt withdrawal of this stimulant, which he had come to rely upon, did more harm than good. His pupils now began to arrive in Bayreuth— Stavenhagen, Siloti and Sophie Menter among them. They were mystified by the situation. Cosima had banned all visitors and they hovered outside, uncertain what to do. On the 27th, Liszt took a turn for the worse, but Cosima, who was busy supervising a reception to be held in Wahnfried that evening, was unable to attend him. Nobody seems to have been aware of his plight. On the Wednesday, Liszt's condition was so grave that even Cosima became alarmed and summoned a second doctor. Pneumonia was diagnosed. Although there were plenty of willing helpers, including Lina Schmalhausen and Adelheid von Schorn, two devoted pupils, Cosima would brook no interference and they were summarily dismissed. Lina defied Cosima's ban; she visited Liszt in his room the following day and was shocked by his condition. Next day, Friday, Liszt became delirious. It was midnight before the doctor was called again, and later still when Cosima returned from the theatre. Another doctor was called in on Saturday, 31 July, and Cosima, warned that her father's last hour was approaching, spent the day at his bedside. His condition slowly deteriorated and he went into a coma. At 10.30 p.m. he was heard to whisper 'Tristan'. Fifteen minutes later he was dead.

His body was left in the lodging house for a time, but as the other guests objected it was transferred to the Villa Wahnfried. Liszt's pupils were outraged by the lack of respect shown to their master. Liszt had not even been given extreme unction. The crowning touch to the tragedy came when the parish minister, a Protestant and a Lutheran, was called in to pronounce the benediction over the remains of Liszt, an Abbé in the Roman Catholic

Wagner welcomes Liszt

Church. The funeral was on 3 August. Liszt's wishes, contained in his Will, were not carried out. He was not given a Requiem Mass, nor was he buried in the habit of the Order of St. Francis. Walter Bache, who dashed from London in two days to be present at the funeral, was appalled beyond measure at the levity of the crowds which lined the streets to watch the cortège go by. Everybody was in a gay mood, many of the 'mourners' being casual visitors to the Wagner festival who had come to the funeral merely out of curiosity.

So all Bayreuth celebrated Wagner while Liszt was lowered into the ground. And perhaps this is how Liszt himself would have wished it.

Suggestions for Further Reading

The number of good books on Liszt in the English language is very small. English biographers have not been attracted to him. This is strange in view of his remarkable life which reads like a novel. It is undeniable, however, that there was until recently in this country an almost puritanical aversion to the man and his music. This was all part of the general reaction that the 'objective' twentieth century experienced against the 'subjective' nineteenth century. Happily, this situation is now changing, and there are more hopeful signs of a genuine resurgence of interest in Liszt. Meanwhile, his recent lack of popularity here is reflected in the paucity of literature about him.

By far the most thorough biography of Liszt is by Sacheverell Sitwell; it is a highly informative work which casts many interesting sidelights on the lesser known aspects of Liszt's complex personality. In its discussion of the music, however, it is weak, and for this Humphrey Searle's *The Music of Liszt* can be recommended. Another good book is Walter Beckett's study of Liszt and his music in the 'Master Musician' series. One of the best accounts of Liszt's later works, some of them only recently published, is *The Twilight of Liszt* by the Hungarian scholar Bence Szabolcsi. For a comprehensive study of Liszt and his works, perhaps I may be allowed to mention a symposium *Franz Liszt: the Man and his Music* edited by myself.

Two volumes which are not directly concerned with Liszt, but which illuminate the times in which he lived in a fascinating way are *Paganini of Genoa* by Lillian Day and *The Great Pianists* by Harold Schonberg. I have found both books a stimulating incentive in the writing of my own study, and I am happy to acknowledge my debt to them.

A.W.

Summary of Liszt's Works

There are more than 1,300 works by Liszt. The following outline is intended merely as a brief guide to his total output.

Piano

Piano Sonata
Three Concertos (including *Totentanz*)
Twelve Transcendental Studies
Six '*Paganini*' *Studies*
Miscellaneous Concert Studies (including 'Leggierezza', 'Gnomenreigen', and 'Waldesrauschen', etc.)
Years of Pilgrimage, in 3 volumes, 26 pieces (including three Petrarch Sonnets, 'Dante' Sonata, and *Les jeux d'eau à la Villa d'Este*)
Harmonies poétiques et religieuses, 10 pieces (including *Funérailles* and *Bénédiction de Dieu*)
Nineteen *Hungarian Rhapsodies*
Three *Mephisto* Waltzes
More than 70 Operatic Paraphrases (including *Norma*, *Don Juan* and *Rigoletto*)
More than 100 Transcriptions (including Beethoven's nine symphonies and Berlioz's *Fantastic* Symphony)
Dozens of miscellaneous works (including the *Weinen, Klagen* variations, six *Consolations*, three *Liebesträume*, *Hungarian Historical Portraits*, etc., etc.)

Orchestral

Thirteen Symphonic Poems
Two Symphonies ('Dante' and 'Faust')
Three Funeral Odes

Two Episodes from Lenau's *Faust*
Miscellaneous Transcriptions (including some of Liszt's own Hungarian
Rhapsodies)

Vocal

Seventy Songs
Ninety Sacred and Secular Choral works (including the Oratorios *Christus*
and *St. Elisabeth*)

Organ

Twenty-one miscellaneous works (including the Fantasy and Fugue on
Meyerbeer's *Ad nos, ad salutarem undam* and the Prelude and Fugue on
the name B.A.C.H.)

Other Music

There is a vast quantity of music for various combinations of chamber
instruments, piano duet, two pianos, songs with orchestra, etc.

Literary Works

Liszt wrote on a great variety of artistic topics all his life. His literary
works are published in seven volumes. They include letters, articles,
essays, some of which are of great historical interest and throw considerable light on his music.

Liszt's Editions of other Composers' Works

Liszt brought out several editions of works by other composers in whom
he was particularly interested, including Chopin's Studies, Bach's Chromatic Fantasy and John Field's Nocturnes.

A Selection of Recordings

Liszt died in 1886, eight years after Thomas Edison invented the phonograph. In theory, then, he could easily have made one of those early wax-cylinder recordings and settled, once and for all, the vexed question: 'What was Liszt *really* like as a pianist?' We may be thankful that the opportunity was never presented to him. The legend of Liszt's playing has remained untarnished by the many technical shortcomings of the earliest gramophone records, which marred the posthumous reputations even of such giants of the keyboard as Busoni and Paderewski. Liszt has left us a far greater evidence of his all-embracing powers as a pianist in his vast output for the piano, which was first brought to life under his own ten fingers, and which tells us more about his art than could a hundred discs.

Piano Solo

12 Transcendental Studies (complete)
> Louis Kentner
>> Turnabout TV 34224 (s)
> György Cziffra
>> H.M.V. ALP 1816

Six 'Paganini' Studies (complete)
> Nikita Magaloff
>> Philips A 00456 L
> Alfred Brendel
>> Vox PL 10800
> Gary Graffman
>> R.C.A. SB 2118 (s)

Hungarian Rhapsodies
> (Nos. 2, 3, 8, 13, 15, 17)
> Alfred Brendel
>> Vanguard VSL 11070 (s)

A Selection of Recordings

Six Consolations (complete)
> Peter Katin
>> Decca LXT 2877
> Edith Farnadi
>> H.M.V. XLP 20084

Sonata in B minor
> Emil Gilels
>> R.C.A. Victor SB 6678 (s)
> Artur Rubinstein
>> R.C.A. Victor SB 6667 (s)
> Clifford Curzon
>> Decca SXL 6076 (s)
> Alfred Brendel
>> Vox PL 12150

Mephisto Waltz No. 1
> Vladimir Ashkenazy
>> Columbia 33 CX 1813
> Artur Rubinstein
>> R.C.A. Victor LM 1905 C

Ballade No. 2, in B minor
> Edith Farnadi
>> H.M.V. CLP 1751
> Louis Kentner
>> Turnabout TV 34225 (s)

Polonaise No. 2, in E major
> György Cziffra
>> Philips AL 3465
> John Ogdon
>> H.M.V. ASD 2416 (s)

Rhapsodie espagnole
> György Cziffra
>> H.M.V. ALP 1534
> David Wilde
>> H.M.V. HQS 1172 (s)

Piano and Orchestra

Concerto No. 1, in E flat major
> Sviatoslav Richter
>> with London Symphony Orchestra
>> conducted by Kyril Kondrashin
>>> Philips SABL 207 (s)
> Martha Argerich
>> with London Symphony Orchestra
>> conducted by Claudio Abbado
>>> D.G.G. SLPM 139383 (s)
> Artur Rubinstein
>> with R.C.A. Victor Orchestra
>> conducted by Alfred Wallenstein
>>> H.M.V. ALP 1413

Concerto No. 2, in A major
> Byron Janis
>> with Moscow Radio Symphony Orchestra
>> conducted by Gennady Rozhdestvensky
>>> Philips SFM 23004 (s)
> Leonard Pennario
>> with London Symphony Orchestra
>> conducted by René Leibowitz
>>> R.C.A. Victrola VICS 1426 (s)
> Sviatoslav Richter
>> with London Symphony Orchestra
>> conducted by Kyril Kondrashin
>>> Philips SABL 207 (s)

Totentanz: paraphrase on the 'Dies Irae'
> Byron Janis
>> with Chicago Symphony Orchestra
>> conducted by Fritz Reiner
>>> R.C.A. Victrola VICS 1205 (s)
> Peter Katin
>> with London Philharmonic Orchestra
>> conducted by Jean Martinon
>>> Decca ACL 156

Index

Index

Index